GOOD
FOOD
BOOK

Printed in the United States of America.
First Printing, 2018.

Design by Sam Booker
Edited by Geraldine Martin-Coppola and Merce Muse

ISBN: 978-1-64467-582-3

Tastemade, Inc.
3019 Olympic Boulevard
Stage C
Santa Monica, CA 90404

GOOD FOOD BOOK

TASTEMADE ®

Contents

A Note From Tastemade

Tastemade was created to challenge expectations in the world of food, home and travel. This curated collection of our favorite recipes will help you reimagine everyday moments — whether you are making breakfast at home, hosting your first formal dinner party, or cooking for an impromptu gathering with friends.

Within these pages you will find creative and original ideas for dishes that are meant to delight; astonishingly decadent and mouthwatering recipes that will fill you and your friends with awe; flavors inspired from our studios all over the world; and upgraded classics that will elevate any get-together.

All the recipes in this book are linked by one common theme: it's all good food, meant to be shared among family and friends, from backyard Juicy Lucy hamburgers on the grill to intimate dinner parties over crumbs of banoffee pie. These recipes are designed to transport you, and we hope they will inspire you to reimagine how you and your loved ones connect with food.

-The Tastemade Team

Scan to Watch

Center your phone's camera on the QR codes at the corners of the recipes to see them come to life via Tastemade.com or the Tastemade app

Around the Tastemade Table
Slowing Down for the Moments That Matter

Morning Moments

- There's no better feeling than starting a morning with warm homemade bread. We love the perfect bake we get with the **Spring Oven** [13].

- The precision temperature index on our **Fellow kettle** [5] creates the perfect brew! For the best extraction, we brew our black tea at 212°F, coffee at 205°F and green tea at 185°F.

- The adorable **Äggcøddler** [7] allows for breakfast to be assembled the night before. It's the perfect vessel for soft-cooked eggs! We take ours with crème fraiche, chopped ham and a sprinkling of chives. Try a dollop of mashed potatoes underneath for an even creamier bite!

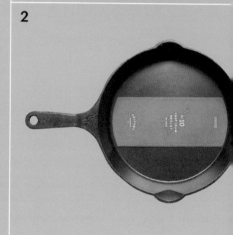

Gatherings With Friends

- Our top dinner party tip? Take the pressure off by pre-cooking steaks in the **Nomiku sous vide circulator** [4]. We use the **Kilner butter churner** [14] to flavor our own butters and then let guests choose their favorite, all while we give a final sear to each steak on the grill.

- Our **Smithey cast iron pan** [2] is the best way to make pizza at home. Turned upside down, it makes for a perfect pizza stone — creating the crispy crust that's so elusive when baking pizza at home. Preheat the pan in a 450 to 500°F oven for about 30 minutes before sliding your pizza on top to bake.

- When friends are over for drinks (often times sipping on a homebrewed **Brooklyn Brew Shop IPA** [12] or home-infused **Camp Craft Cocktail**), we smoke sausages in the **UchiCook tabletop smoker** [1] for easy snacking! Arrange a fruit and cheese board on an **artisanal cutting board** [8] and you've got an easy — but impressive — feast.

- The best hangover hack? Purifying your wine before you even take a sip. Sulfites can be a shortcut to a headache, so we rely on our **ULLO wine purifier** [9] to filter sulfites and sediments, bringing wine back to its natural state.

Sweet Treats

- When pouring yourself a cup of coffee or tea, grab a **stroopwafel** [10] and place it on top of the mug. The trapped steam warms the cookie and softens the caramel filling, making every coffee break that much sweeter.

- We love making store-bought pies and cakes look more sophisticated by presenting them on a **Mosser cake stand** [3] — one of the loveliest objects in our kitchen! Try serving the slices with the **Sagaform gold cake server** [11] for an added dose of elegance.

- Keeping a **Chef'n ice cream maker** [15] on hand means instant ice cream, whenever the craving strikes! Store a basic custard recipe in the fridge and whip up a fresh batch of ice cream in less time than it takes to run to the store for a pint of your favorite flavor.

- It may seem intimidating, but you can learn to bake the perfect macarons with **Dana's Bakery Macaron kit** [6]! Baking and assembling these are a great activity for when friends are over, or for a casual weekend afternoon when your sweet tooth kicks in.

Mornings

Breakfast is best enjoyed with a warm cup of coffee in hand, and when it's finally calm enough to linger around the table with the people you cherish most. Skip the long line at brunch and make one of these recipes instead. Cooking breakfast gives you an opportunity to set the tone for the day — whether you're looking to get creative, indulgent, or go with something cozy and comforting.

Blue Pancakes

Active Time   *25 minutes*
Total Time   *·25 minutes*
Yield   *4 servings*

Ingredients

2 1/4 cups all-purpose flour
3 teaspoons baking powder
2 tablespoons blue spirulina powder
Pinch of salt
3 tablespoons honey
2 large eggs, room temperature
1 3/4 cups whole milk, room temperature
3 tablespoons melted butter, plus more
for cooking
1/2 cup chocolate syrup, to serve
1 cup blueberries, to serve
1 cup mini chocolate chips, to serve

In a large bowl, whisk together the flour, baking powder, spiralina and salt.

In a medium bowl, whisk together the honey, eggs, milk and butter. Pour this mixture into the dry ingredients and mix until just combined.

Heat a skillet over medium-low heat. Brush with a bit of butter. Pour about 1/4 cup of batter onto the hot skillet and cook for about 2 to 4 minutes on each side.

To serve, stack pancakes, pour over chocolate syrup and garnish with blueberries and chocolate chips.

Gravy-Stuffed Biscuits

Active Time *20 minutes*
Total Time *1 hour*
Yield *8 biscuits*

Ingredients

FOR THE GRAVY:

1 tablespoon olive oil
1 small yellow onion, diced
1 pound ground pork sausage
6 tablespoons all-purpose flour
2 1/2 cups whole milk
4 packages gelatin
1/2 teaspoon chopped fresh thyme
1/4 teaspoon chopped fresh sage
1/2 teaspoon cayenne
1 teaspoon salt
1 teaspoon black pepper

FOR THE BISCUITS:

1 (16-ounce) can biscuits
1 large egg, beaten

MAKE THE GRAVY:
Spray an ice cube tray with cooking spray.

In a large cast-iron skillet over medium heat, add oil and saute onion until translucent. Add ground sausage and cook until golden. Once done, sprinkle with flour and stir until the grease from the sausage thickens. Stir in milk. Add gelatin, then mix in thyme, sage, cayenne, salt and pepper.

Fill the ice cube tray with the gravy and refrigerate for 30 minutes.

ASSEMBLE THE BISCUITS:
Preheat oven to 350°F and line a baking sheet with parchment paper.

Split the 8 biscuits in half crosswise and place on the prepared baking sheet. Place a cube of gravy in the middle of each biscuit half and cover with the other half of the biscuit. Seal each biscuit completely by pinching around the edges.

Brush biscuits with egg wash, top with freshly ground pepper and bake for 12 to 15 minutes, or until golden. Serve immediately.

French Toast Bowls

Active Time *30 minutes*
Total Time *30 minutes*
Yield *2 servings*

Ingredients

FOR THE FRENCH TOAST:

2 large eggs
1/3 cup milk
1/4 cup plus 1 tablespoon granulated sugar, divided
2 teaspoons cinnamon, divided
1 small unsliced loaf white sandwich bread
Butter, for frying

FOR THE FILLING:

1/2 cup whipped cream
Strawberries, mango, and kiwi, thinly sliced
Honey, to serve

MAKE THE FRENCH TOAST:
In a small bowl, whisk together the eggs, milk, 1 tablespoon sugar and 1 teaspoon cinnamon until well combined.

Divide loaf into two and remove the crust on all sides. Each piece should resemble a large cube. Cut a square out of the center of each cube, leaving a ½-inch border on all four sides and at the bottom, and remove excess bread in the center to create a bowl. Dip each bread bowl into the egg mixture and turn to coat all sides.

In a frying pan over medium heat, melt a tablespoon of butter and cook bread for 2 minutes on each side until crispy and golden.

Combine the remaining 1 teaspoon cinnamon and remaining ¼ cup sugar in a small bowl. While still warm, dip all the sides in the cinnamon and sugar mixture.

ASSEMBLE THE BOWLS:
Fill French toast bowls with the cream and fruit in alternating layers. Decorate with extra fruit and cream and serve warm with a drizzle of honey on top.

Everything Bagel Croissants

Active Time *1 hour*
Total Time *2 hours*
Yield *12 croissants*

Ingredients

FOR THE FILLING:

2 cups cream cheese, softened
1/2 cup chopped scallions
1/4 cup chopped chives
1 tablespoon lemon juice
1/2 teaspoon salt

FOR THE TOPPING:

2 tablespoons sesame seeds
1 tablespoon poppy seeds
1 tablespoon large flake salt
2 teaspoons dried onion flakes
2 teaspoons dried garlic flakes

FOR THE CROISSANTS:

6 sheets puff pastry dough, thawed
1 large egg, beaten

MAKE THE FILLING:
In a large bowl, combine cream cheese, scallions, chives, lemon juice and salt.

MAKE THE TOPPING:
In a small bowl, stir together sesame seeds, poppy seeds, salt, onion and garlic flakes.

ASSEMBLE THE CROISSANTS:
Preheat oven to 400°F and line a baking sheet with parchment paper.

Divide each puff pastry sheet into two pieces lengthwise. Fold each strip in half crosswise to form a square and roll out slightly to create extra flaky layers. Place 3 tablespoons of cream cheese filling in the center and roll over onto itself to enclose the filling and create a log shape. Brush with egg and top with seed mixture.

Bake for 15 to 20 minutes, or until golden and crispy. Croissants are best served day of.

Strawberry Popovers with Butter and Compote

Active Time *25 minutes*
Total Time *1 hour*
Yield *6 popovers*

Ingredients

FOR THE POPOVERS:

3 large eggs
1 1/4 cups whole milk
1 1/4 cups all-purpose flour
1/4 teaspoon fine sea salt
1 tablespoon unsalted butter, melted
1 1/2 tablespoons unsalted butter, cut evenly into 6 pieces
1/4 cup sliced strawberries

FOR THE STRAWBERRY COMPOTE:

2 cups strawberries
2 tablespoons water
1/2 cup sugar

FOR THE THYME BUTTER:

1 cup (2 sticks) butter, room temperature
2 teaspoons fresh thyme leaves
1 teaspoon sea salt

MAKE THE POPOVERS:
Preheat oven to 425°F.

In a large mixing bowl, whisk the eggs until they become pale yellow and voluminous. Whisk in the milk. Gradually add the flour and salt and continue to whisk until the mixture is smooth and creamy. Whisk in the melted butter.

Preheat a 6-cup popover pan or 12-cup muffin tin in the oven for 2 minutes.

Place one piece of butter in each cup and return pan to oven for another minute. Butter should be melted and bubbly.

Divide the batter evenly among the cups and place in sliced strawberries. Bake for 20 minutes.

Without opening the oven, lower the heat to 325°F and bake for another 20 minutes. Popovers should be puffed and golden brown. (To avoid deflating the popovers, use the oven light rather than opening the oven door to check on them.)

Serve warm with a smear of thyme butter and a spoonful of strawberry compote.

MAKE THE STRAWBERRY COMPOTE:
In a wide saucepan, combine the strawberries, water and sugar. Cook over medium low heat until the sugar is dissolved and the strawberries begin to soften and break down, about 10 minutes, stirring occasionally.

Transfer to a storage jar and set aside to cool to room temperature. The compote will keep for one week when stored in an airtight container in the fridge.

MAKE THE THYME BUTTER:
In a small bowl, mix together butter, thyme and salt. Store in an airtight jar.

Lur

ch + Dinner

With creative preparations and bold flavors, these are new classics to warm your home and easily serve a crowd. This chapter will inspire you to throw more lunch and dinner parties, and give you the confidence to step out of your comfort zone when it comes to entertaining at home.

Rustic Tomato Pie

Active Time *30 minutes*
Total Time *2 hours 20 minutes*
Yield *8 to 10 servings*

—

Ingredients

FOR THE DOUGH:

2 3/4 cups all-purpose flour
1 tablespoon sugar
1 1/2 teaspoons kosher salt
1 cup plus 2 tablespoons unsalted
butter, cubed and chilled
6 tablespoons ice water

FOR THE PIE:

3 tablespoons stone-ground mustard
1 cup sharp white cheddar cheese,
grated
Kosher salt and freshly ground pepper
3 to 4 pints ripe tomatoes of various
sizes, colors and shapes
1 large egg, beaten
4 to 6 fresh thyme sprigs
Large-flake sea salt

MAKE THE DOUGH:

In the bowl of a food processor, place flour, sugar and salt and pulse to combine. Add butter to the processor and pulse until the mixture resembles a coarse meal. With the processor running, slowly drizzle in up to 6 tablespoons of ice water until the mixture comes together and begins to form a ball. Knead the dough a few times by hand if necessary, so it comes together, then wrap in plastic wrap. Refrigerate for at least one hour.

MAKE THE PIE:

Preheat oven to 375°F and line a baking sheet with parchment paper.

Roll out dough to a circle about ¼-inch thick. Spread mustard and sprinkle cheese all over the dough, leaving a 2-inch border around the edge. Season with a bit of salt and pepper.

Chop larger tomatoes in pieces or slices, medium tomatoes in half and leave small cherry tomatoes whole. Place tomatoes over the cheese layer and fold the edges of the crust inwards over the filling. Make sure to seal the cracks that appear, then brush crust with egg wash. Sprinkle all over with thyme leaves and large-flake sea salt. Bake for 30 to 35 minutes, until crust is golden and filling is bubbling.

Allow to cool for 15 to 20 minutes, then slice and serve warm.

Homemade Chicken Shawarma

Active Time *20 minutes*
Total Time *2 hours*
Yield *4 to 6 servings*

—

Ingredients

FOR THE MARINADE:

1 cup Greek-style yogurt
Juice of 2 lemons
1 tablespoon ground cumin
1 tablespoon za'atar
1 teaspoon smoked paprika
1 teaspoon turmeric
1 teaspoon garlic powder
1/2 teaspoon cayenne pepper
Salt and pepper, to taste

FOR THE SHAWARMA:

8 boneless, skinless chicken thighs, pounded flat
1 large red onion
Large skewer
Pita, to serve
Tabbouleh, to serve
Tzatziki, to serve
Grilled tomatoes, to serve
Lemon wedges, to serve

MAKE THE MARINADE:
In a large bowl, combine yogurt, lemon juice, cumin, za'atar, paprika, turmeric, garlic powder, cayenne, salt and pepper. Add chicken thighs and mix to coat. Cover and refrigerate for 1 hour.

MAKE THE SHAWARMA:
Preheat oven to 400°F.

Cut a large red onion in half crosswise. Remove the skin and place one half face down on a baking sheet. Insert the skewer into the onion, vertically like a spit. Layer each chicken thigh on the skewer, piercing through the center of each, until they are all stacked on top of each other. Place the other onion half on top of the skewer. Bake for 1 hour, or until cooked through to an internal temperature of 165°F.

Use a sharp knife to carve off slices of chicken. Serve with pita and other sides.

Salt-Crusted Chicken

Active Time *30 minutes*
Total Time *5 hours 30 minutes*
Yield *4 servings*

—

Ingredients

FOR THE BRINE:

1 head garlic, halved crosswise
1 tablespoon salt
1 teaspoon freshly ground black pepper
1 tablespoon olive oil
1/2 large lemon
2 tablespoons balsamic vinegar
2 bay leaves
4 cups water

FOR THE CHICKEN:

1 (3 to 4 pound) chicken
1/2 large lemon
2 sprigs tarragon
2 sprigs thyme
7 cups kosher salt
10 large egg whites

MAKE THE BRINE:
In a large pot over high heat, combine garlic, salt, pepper, olive oil, halved lemon, vinegar, bay leaves and water. Bring to boil. Remove the brine from heat and cool to room temperature. Once the brine is cooled, submerge the chicken. Refrigerate covered for at least 4 hours.

BAKE THE CHICKEN:
Preheat oven to 350°F.

Remove the chicken from the brine and pat dry. Place the lemon half, tarragon and thyme into the chicken cavity and truss with kitchen twine. Discard the brine.

In a large bowl, combine the salt and egg whites. Place one-third of the mixture into an 8-by-10 ½-inch roasting dish. Nestle the chicken on top of the salt and cover with remaining salt mix until fully coated.

Roast for 1 hour and 10 minutes or until the salt is hard and dry. Set aside to rest for 15 minutes before cracking off the salt. The skin will be very salty, but the meat underneath will not. Make sure to peel away the skin to reveal the juicy and tender meat underneath.

Pineapple-Roasted Chicken

Active Time *30 minutes*
Total Time *1 hour 45 minutes*
Yield *4 servings*

—

Ingredients

1/4 cup soy sauce
1/3 cup brown sugar
1/3 cup pineapple juice
1 tablespoon garlic paste
1 tablespoon ginger paste
1 large pineapple
1 (2 1/2 to 3 pound) free-range chicken
1 avocado, peeled, pitted and cubed
1/2 cup red onions, diced
1 red chili, thinly sliced
Juice of 1/2 lime

In a medium saucepan over medium-high heat, add soy sauce, brown sugar, pineapple juice, garlic and ginger. Stir, and bring to a boil. Reduce heat and let simmer for 5 minutes until it starts to thicken. Set aside to cool.

Preheat oven to 425°F.

Trim the top from the pineapple. Cut a slice from the bottom so it stands level. Cut vertical slices from the pineapple all around the core, stopping 2 to 3 inches from the base of the pineapple. You'll be left with the vertical core of the pineapple on a 2- or 3-inch base, forming the "stand" for the chicken. Place it upright in a baking tray. Position the chicken on the pineapple, then brush it with marinade. Reserve the unused pineapple for the salsa.

Roast for 15 minutes, then baste with leftover marinade. Reduce oven temperature to 375°F and cook for another 45 minutes, basting with marinade occasionally.

Meanwhile, dice the remaining pineapple flesh and add to a medium bowl with avocado, red onions, chili and lime.

When cooked through to an internal temperature of 165°F, turn oven off and leave the door ajar for 10 minutes to let the chicken rest before serving alongside salsa.

Moroccan-Style Sliders with Harissa Mayo

Active Time *30 minutes*
Total Time *1 hour 5 minutes*
Yield *12 sliders*

—

Ingredients

FOR THE CARROT PICKLES:

1 bunch small carrots, thinly sliced
3 sprigs fresh dill
1/2 cup water
1/2 cup rice vinegar
3 tablespoons sugar
2 1/2 teaspoons kosher salt

FOR THE HARISSA MAYO:

1/3 cup mayonnaise
2 teaspoons harissa
1 teaspoon lemon juice

FOR THE SLIDERS:

1 pound ground beef
1/2 cup panko breadcrumbs
1 small onion, minced
1 teaspoon ground cumin
1/2 teaspoon cinnamon
1/2 teaspoon ground coriander
Pinch of cayenne pepper
1 large egg
1 teaspoon kosher salt
1 (12-count) tray sweet Hawaiian rolls
1 tablespoon butter, melted
Dried onion

MAKE THE PICKLES:
Place carrots and dill in a heatproof jar. In a medium pot, combine water, vinegar, sugar and salt and bring to a boil. Allow to cool slightly, then pour over the carrots. Set aside to cool.

MAKE THE HARISSA MAYO:
In a small bowl, whisk together the mayo, harissa and lemon juice; refrigerate until ready to use.

MAKE THE SLIDERS:
Preheat oven to 375°F and line a baking sheet with parchment paper.

In a medium bowl, combine the beef, breadcrumbs, onion, cumin, cinnamon, coriander, cayenne, egg and salt, taking care not to overmix. Form into 12 patties, place on the prepared baking sheet and bake for 20 to 25 minutes.

Place a new sheet of parchment paper on the baking sheet.

Slice the Hawaiian rolls in half crosswise. Remove the top half of the sheet. Place the bottom half on the prepared baking sheet. Spread mayo mixture all over and place a burger on each square. Top with pickled carrots. Place the roll tops on top and brush all over with butter. Sprinkle with dried onion and bake for 7 to 9 minutes, until warmed through. Serve immediately.

Feta-Stuffed Meatballs

Active Time *25 minutes*
Total Time *45 minutes*
Yield *4 servings*

—

Ingredients

FOR THE MEATBALLS:

1 1/2 pounds lean ground beef
3 green onions, thinly sliced
1 large egg
2 tablespoons chopped mint
2 cloves garlic, minced
1 teaspoon ground cumin
Kosher salt and freshly ground black pepper
1 (3-ounce) block feta, cut into 1/2-inch cubes

FOR THE SPICED CHICKPEAS:

3 tablespoons extra-virgin olive oil
6 cloves garlic, thinly sliced
1 shallot, sliced
2 teaspoons smoked paprika
1 teaspoon ground cumin
Pinch of red chili flakes
Kosher salt and freshly ground pepper
2 (15-ounce) cans chickpeas, drained and rinsed
1/4 cup cilantro leaves

FOR THE ZUCCHINI NOODLES:

4 spiralized zucchinis
2 tablespoons olive oil
Juice of 1/2 lemon
Pinch kosher salt

FOR SERVING:

Feta cheese
Grated carrots
Grape tomatoes, sliced
Persian-style cucumbers, sliced

MAKE THE MEATBALLS:
Preheat oven to 425°F and line a sheet tray with parchment paper.

Combine beef, green onions, egg, mint, garlic, cumin, salt and pepper in a large bowl. Roll golf ball-sized meatballs with your hands and pop a cube of feta inside. Bake for 15 to 20 minutes.

MAKE THE CHICKPEAS:
Add olive oil to a large skillet over medium-high heat. Once hot, add garlic and shallot and sauté until softened, about 4 minutes. Sprinkle with smoked paprika, cumin and chili flakes. Stir until fragrant, about 1 minute. Season with a pinch of salt and pepper. Stir in chickpeas and cook for 5 minutes. Taste for seasoning and adjust. Turn off heat and stir in cilantro leaves.

MAKE THE ZUCCHINI NOODLES:
Add zucchini to a bowl and drizzle with olive oil, lemon juice and salt. Toss with hands. Let soften for 5 to 10 minutes at room temperature.

ASSEMBLE THE BOWL
Add zucchini noodles to the bottom of the bowl, top with meatballs, spiced chickpeas, feta, grated carrots, sliced grape tomatoes and sliced cucumbers.

Thai Shaking Beef with Red Onion and Cucumber

Active Time *25 minutes*
Prep Time *1 hour 30 minutes*
Yield *2 servings*

—

Ingredients

FOR THE RED ONION AND CUCUMBER SALAD:

1/4 cup sugar
1/4 cup rice vinegar
2 tablespoons water
1/2 tablespoon chili-garlic sauce
Pinch of salt
1 English cucumber, sliced
1/4 red onion, thinly sliced
1 tablespoon cilantro
Handful of peanuts (optional)

FOR THE STEAK:

1 bone-in porterhouse steak, 2 pounds and about 1 1/2-inches thick
3 cloves garlic, minced
2 tablespoons vegetable oil
Pinch of salt
1 tablespoon sugar
1/4 cup rice vinegar
2 tablespoons soy sauce
1 tablespoon fish sauce
Pinch of pepper
2 cloves garlic, smashed
2 tablespoons butter
Plum tomatoes, sliced into wedges, to serve
Jasmine rice, cooked, to serve

MAKE THE SALAD:
In a small saucepan, combine sugar, rice vinegar, water, chili-garlic sauce and salt. Bring to a simmer or until sugar has dissolved. Set aside to cool slightly. In a medium-sized mixing bowl, combine sugar vinegar mixture, cucumber, red onion and cilantro. Refrigerate for at least one hour. When ready to serve, toss in peanuts, if using.

MARINATE THE STEAK:
Rub the steak with garlic, oil and salt. Set aside and marinate for at least one hour.

COOK THE STEAK:
In a small bowl, combine sugar, rice vinegar, soy sauce, fish sauce and pepper. Set sauce aside until ready to use.

Heat a heavy-bottomed skillet to smoking. Add the steak, let it sit and sear until a nice crust forms, about 7 minutes. Flip and sear. Drop in butter and smashed garlic; baste steak for 4 minutes. Pour in the sauce, coating the steak. Remove and rest for 5 minutes before slicing.

Serve steak with red onion and cucumber salad, tomatoes and rice.

Sheet Pan Steak Frites

Active Time *30 minutes*
Total Time *45 minutes*
Yield *2 servings*

—

Ingredients

FOR THE SHALLOT AND THYME BUTTER:

2 sticks unsalted butter, room temperature
2 teaspoons fresh thyme leaves
1/4 cup minced shallots
Salt and pepper, to taste
1 teaspoon red wine vinegar

FOR THE STEAK FRITES:

Vegetable oil
2 russet potatoes, cut lengthwise into 8 wedges
2 tablespoons olive oil
1/2 cup freshly grated Parmesan
Salt and pepper, to taste
2 New York strip steaks, about 1 pound each

MAKE THE SHALLOT AND THYME BUTTER:
In a medium bowl, cream the butter with a fork. Mix in thyme, shallot, salt, pepper and vinegar. Place on a sheet of plastic wrap and roll tightly into a log. Refrigerate overnight or until firm.

COOK THE STEAK FRITES:
Preheat oven to 350°F and generously oil a baking sheet with vegetable oil.

Place potatoes in a single layer on one side of the prepared baking sheet. Add olive oil and Parmesan cheese, season with salt and pepper and gently toss to combine. Bake for 20 to 25 minutes, tossing occasionally.

Remove pan from the oven and preheat to broil.

Season both steaks with salt and pepper and place on the opposite side of the baking sheet. Place in oven and broil until the steak is browned and charred at the edges, about 4 to 5 minutes per side until desired doneness. Garnish with parsley and serve immediately with shallot and thyme butter.

Juicy Lucy Crunch Burger

Active Time *50 minutes*
Total Time *1 hour 20 minutes*
Yield *4 burgers*

—

Ingredients

FOR THE CHIPS:

2 pounds fingerling potatoes, washed and chilled
1 tablespoon white vinegar
4 cups vegetable oil for deep-frying
1 teaspoon seasoned salt

FOR THE SAUCE:

1/4 cup mayonnaise
1 teaspoon dill pickle juice
1 teaspoon diced mini dill pickles
2 teaspoons ketchup
1 teaspoon yellow mustard
1/4 teaspoon smoked paprika
1/4 teaspoon onion powder
1/4 teaspoon garlic powder
1/2 teaspoon minced parsley leaves

FOR THE BURGERS:

2 slices mild cheddar cheese, quartered
2 slices American cheese, quartered
1 1/2 pounds ground chuck, chilled
1 teaspoon seasoned salt
1/2 teaspoon onion powder
1/2 teaspoon Worcestershire sauce
1/4 teaspoon black pepper
Brioche buns, green leaf lettuce and tomato, to serve

FRY THE CHIPS:

Using a mandoline, slice each potato into paper-thin rounds. Transfer the slices to a bowl of ice water. Add vinegar to the sliced potatoes. Drain on paper towels and allow to dry for at least 30 minutes.

In a 3-quart shallow saucepan, heat oil until a deep-fat thermometer registers 380°F. Working in batches of 10 or 12 slices, fry potatoes until golden, about 2 minutes. Transfer chips to a baking sheet lined with paper towels and sprinkle with seasoned salt.

MAKE THE SAUCE:

In a small bowl, whisk together the mayo, pickle juice, minced pickles, ketchup, mustard, paprika, onion powder, garlic powder and parsley.

COOK THE BURGERS:

Preheat a grill pan or outdoor grill to medium-high heat.

Stack 2 quarters of American cheese on top of 2 quarters of cheddar cheese. Repeat with remaining cheese slices.

In a large bowl, place the ground chuck and add the seasoned salt, onion powder, Worcestershire and black pepper. Mix with your hands until just combined. Do not overwork the meat mixture.

Divide the meat into 8 equal portions. Using your fingers, press 2 portions of the meat into 2 ¼-inch-thick patties that are each about 1-inch wider than the hamburger buns. Place a stack of cheese into the center of one patty and place the second patty on top, making sure to pinch and round off the edges carefully. Repeat with remaining portions. Cook each stuffed patty for about 4 minutes on each side and allow to rest before serving.

To assemble the burgers, spread about 1 tablespoon of sauce on both sides of a brioche bun. Place the bottom bun on a clean plate. Layer the lettuce, then the burger, followed by a tomato slice and a small handful of chips. Top with the coated top bun. Serve immediately with extra chips and a side of sauce.

Lamb Shank Pot Pie

Active Time *35 minutes*
Total Time *3 hours*
Yield *4 pies*

—

Ingredients

FOR THE FILLING:

2 tablespoons olive oil
4 small to medium lamb shanks
2 small onions, finely chopped
1 carrot, finely chopped
1 celery stalk, finely chopped
2 cloves garlic, peeled
4 anchovy fillets
1 cup red wine
2 sprigs thyme
2 sprigs rosemary
2 cups lamb stock

FOR THE DOUGH:

½ cup plus 1 tablespoon ice cold butter, cubed
2 cups all-purpose flour
4 ounces cream cheese, chilled
1 large egg, beaten
2 tablespoons heavy cream

MAKE THE FILLING:

Heat the oil in a large heavy-bottomed pot over medium heat, then brown the lamb shanks well. Remove from pot and set aside.

Add the onions, carrot, celery and garlic into the casserole and cook gently until soft. Add the anchovies and stir to dissolve into the mixture. Add the red wine and cook for 3 to 4 minutes, stirring and scraping to deglaze the pan. Put the lamb shanks back in the pan with thyme and rosemary, add stock to cover and bring to a boil. Cover with a lid and simmer on low for 1 ½ to 2 hours until the meat is tender. Check a few times to make sure the shanks are still covered with liquid. If not, top the casserole up with more stock.

MAKE THE DOUGH:

In the bowl of a food processor, pulse together the butter and flour until the mixture resembles coarse breadcrumbs. Add the cream cheese and pulse a few times more, until the dough starts to come together. Shape into a disc, about 1-inch thick, then wrap in plastic wrap and chill in the fridge for 30 minutes.

ASSEMBLE THE PIES:

Preheat oven to 400°F.

After 1 ½ to 2 hours, the lamb shanks should be very tender but not yet falling off the bone. Put one lamb shank upright in each 1 ½-cup capacity ramekin or oven-proof bowl, then divide the remaining sauce among the 4 ramekins. Let cool for 15 minutes.

Roll out the dough, just big enough to cut four lids each about 1 inch larger than the top of the ramekins. Cut an X in the middle of each to slide the shank bone through. Slide the lids over the shank bone to fit on top of the pudding tins, with a ½-inch overhang around the edge. Pinch the dough around the edge of the tin to secure it. Cut the dough in a circle around the bone, so that air can escape. Beat together the egg and cream, and brush this egg wash on top of the lids. Bake for 25 minutes until golden brown.

Let the pies cool for five minutes before serving them in their tins.

Tornado Shrimp with Bang Bang Sauce

Active Time *30 minutes*
Total Time *30 minutes*
Yield *4 servings*

—

Ingredients

FOR THE BANG BANG SAUCE:

2/3 cup mayonnaise
1/4 cup Sriracha
1/4 cup sweet chili sauce
1 tablespoon brown sugar
2 tablespoons rice vinegar

FOR THE PRAWNS:

4 cups oil, for deep-frying
1 (17-ounce) package kataifi (shredded phyllo dough)
12 large shrimp, shelled with tail on

MAKE THE SAUCE:
In a small mixing bowl, add mayonnaise, Sriracha, chili sauce, brown sugar and vinegar, and whisk together.

MAKE THE SHRIMP:
In a deep-sided, heavy-bottomed pot add oil and heat to 350°F.

Remove the dough from its package and place under a damp cloth. Pull a handful of pastry from the pack and tightly wrap it around one shrimp. Cover with a damp cloth and set aside while you repeat with the rest of the shrimp.

When the oil has come to temperature, lower one shrimp at a time into the hot oil and cook for 2 to 3 minutes, or until golden brown. Drain on paper towels and repeat until all of the shrimp are cooked. Serve immediately, with dipping sauce on the side.

Garlic Butter Scallops

Active Time   15 minutes
Total Time   15 minutes
Yield   4 servings

—

Ingredients

FOR THE SCALLOPS:

1 1/2 pounds scallops, about 20 pieces
Sea salt and pepper, to taste
2 tablespoons olive oil

FOR THE SAUCE:

4 tablespoons unsalted butter
5 cloves garlic, minced
1/2 cup white wine
1 cup heavy cream
2 tablespoons lemon juice
Pinch of red pepper flakes
1/4 cup chopped parsley, plus more to garnish
Salt, to taste
1 tablespoon lemon zest

MAKE THE SCALLOPS:

Pat scallops dry with paper towels and season lightly with salt and pepper.

Heat a large nonstick pan over medium-high heat and add olive oil. After 30 seconds, add scallops; do not crowd pan, work in batches if necessary. Sauté until a dark golden, about 2 minutes, then turn and cook other side. When second side is golden, transfer scallops to a platter; cover and keep warm.

MAKE THE SAUCE:

Keeping the pan on medium-high heat, add butter and garlic and saute until fragrant, about 30 seconds. Add white wine to deglaze the pan and finish with heavy cream, lemon juice, red pepper flakes, parsley and salt. Reduce heat to medium-low and return scallops to pan to warm. Top with parsley and lemon zest and serve immediately.

Tuna Poke Tacos

Active Time *20 minutes*
Total Time *30 minutes*
Yield *4 servings*

———

Ingredients

FOR THE TACO SHELLS:

2 cups Thai sticky rice, cooked
Vegetable oil, for cooking

FOR THE FILLING:

1 Ahi Tuna steak, cubed
Sesame seeds
Scallions, thinly sliced
Wasabi paste
Spicy mayo

MAKE THE RICE TACO SHELLS:
Lay out the sticky rice in between 2 sheets of plastic wrap and roll out ¼-inch thick. Using a 4-inch cookie cutter, stamp out 4 rounds.

Heat a teaspoon of oil in a large frying pan set over medium-low heat. Working in batches, cook each on only one side until golden and crispy, about 5 minutes each. Using the back of a muffin pan, with the grilled side facing downwards, shape rice rounds into taco shells in between the ridges of the pan. Set aside for 10 minutes to cool and harden.

ASSEMBLE THE TACOS:
Fill the tacos with the tuna, sesame seeds and scallions. Top with wasabi paste and spicy mayo. Serve immediately.

Puff Pastry Salmon

Active Time *15 minutes*
Total Time *40 minutes*
Yield *1 serving*

—

Ingredients

1/3 cup cream cheese, room temperature
2 teaspoons mayonnaise
1 tablespoon chopped dill, plus more to serve
1 teaspoon chopped oregano
Juice of 1/2 lemon
1 large egg
1 tablespoon milk
1 (6- to 8- ounce) salmon fillet, skin off
Sea salt and pepper, to taste
2 sheets puff pastry, thawed
1 tablespoon whole-grain mustard
1/2 cup steamed spinach, excess liquid squeezed out and discarded

Preheat oven to 400°F and line a baking sheet with parchment paper.

In a medium bowl, stir together cream cheese, mayonnaise, dill, oregano, and lemon juice.

In a small bowl, whisk together egg and milk.

Season salmon with salt and pepper. Spread mustard in the center of 1 sheet of puff pastry and top with spinach, the salmon fillet and cheese mixture. Brush egg wash along the edges of the puff pastry and place another sheet of pastry on top. Shape the pastry into a fish shape, trimming away the excess dough and seal the edges of the pastry with a fork. Reserve excess dough for decorations.

Using a knife, score the pastry all over to create a fish scale design. With the leftover pastry, create a mouth, eye, and fins and attach with egg wash. Bake for 25 minutes, or until golden brown. Garnish with dill before serving.

Herb-Laminated Pasta

Active Time *30 minutes*
Total Time *1 hour*
Yield *about 4 servings*

—

Ingredients

3 large eggs, beaten
2 cups all-purpose flour
1 tablespoon extra-virgin olive oil
Pinch of salt
1 large bunch sage, leaves picked
1 large bunch flat leaf parsley, leaves picked
Semolina flour, for dusting

In the bowl of a stand mixer, combine eggs, flour, oil and salt with your hands until a shaggy dough forms. Knead with dough hook attachment until dough is smooth and elastic, about 10 minutes. Cover dough with plastic wrap and let rest for at least 30 minutes.

Divide the dough into 4 equal portions. Set a pasta machine to the first setting. Lightly dust one portion of the dough with flour, then form it into a rectangle. Pass the pasta through the rollers on setting 1 and repeat the rolling and flouring process so that the pasta passes through setting 1 a total of 3 times.

Change the rollers to setting 2, lightly flour the pasta, then pass it through the rollers. Change the rollers to setting 3, lightly flour the pasta and then pass it through the rollers. Continue with the flouring and rolling until the pasta is passed through setting 6. Repeat the rolling and flouring process with the remaining pieces of dough, placing the rolled out sheets of pasta on the floured baking sheet.

Lay one sheet of pasta flat on the work surface. Arrange the sage and parsley leaves on the dough, leaving space between each leaf. Very lightly dab the edges of the sheet of pasta with water and then carefully lay a second sheet of pasta dough on top of the herbs, enclosing them between the two sheets of dough. Using your hands, lightly press the two sheets together so that they stick. Pass the pasta sheet through the rollers on setting 3 to seal the two sheets together. Repeat the layering and rolling process with the remaining sheets of dough.

Use the full sheets of dough to make filled ravioli or slice into long strips to create pappardelle. Pasta should be cooked in heavily salted boiling water for about 3 minutes, until the pasta rises to the top of the pot.

Mini Mushroom Alfredo Bakes

Active Time *30 minutes*
Total Time *50 minutes*
Yield *2 small skillets*

—

Ingredients

FOR THE ALFREDO SAUCE:

1/2 cup butter
1 cup heavy cream
2 cloves garlic, minced
6 ounces shredded Parmesan cheese
Pinch of nutmeg
Kosher salt, to taste
Freshly ground black pepper, to taste

FOR THE PASTA:

1 pound rigatoni, cooked according to
package instructions and drained
4 cups mixed mushrooms
2 cups shredded mozzarella
Olive oil
Fresh parsley, to serve

MAKE THE SAUCE:

In a small skillet set over medium heat, stir together butter, cream and garlic until butter is melted. Add cheese and stir until smooth. Season with nutmeg, salt and pepper. Set aside to cool slightly.

ASSEMBLE THE PASTA SKILLETS:

Preheat oven to 350°F and grease 2 5-inch single serving-sized cast-iron skillets.

Pour ¼ cup sauce into each skillet. Arrange the rigatoni pieces upright tightly in the skillets; they will look a bit like honeycomb. Pour the remaining sauce over the pasta in each dish. Tap the base of the skillets to allow the sauce to get between the holes, spooning more on if necessary. Place the mushroom stalks into the rigatoni holes. Top with shredded mozzarella and a drizzle of olive oil. Bake for 20 minutes, or until cheese is golden and bubbling. Top with a sprinkling of parsley and serve warm.

Chorizo Manchego Carbonara

Active Time *25 minutes*
Total Time *25 minutes*
Yield *3 servings*

—

Ingredients

1 (6- to 7-pound) Manchego cheese wheel
2 large eggs
1 large egg yolk
3 tablespoons olive oil
1/2 cup diced chorizo
2 cloves garlic, sliced
1/2 teaspoon red pepper flakes
6 ounces spaghetti, cooked al dente
according to package instructions
Salt and pepper, to taste
2 tablespoons parsley, minced
Splash of vodka

Using a cheese plane or a melon baller, shave enough space from the top and center of the cheese wheel to resemble a bowl, leaving walls about 1 to 1 ½-inch thick around the sides and a couple inches deep. Reserve the shaved cheese (about ¾ cup).

In a small bowl, whisk together eggs, yolk and shaved manchego until it forms a paste.

In a frying pan over medium heat, heat oil and cook the chorizo until crispy. Add garlic and cook for 30 seconds, until fragrant and lightly golden. Add red pepper flakes and the cooked pasta, tossing to coat. Remove the pan from the heat, and add salt and pepper to taste. Pour in manchego-egg mixture, add parsley; quickly toss everything together.

Pour a little vodka into the hollowed out cheese bowl and, very carefully, light on fire. Add pasta and toss chorizo carbonara inside of the cheese bowl, coating it with the melted cheese. Serve immediately.

Timpano

Active Time *30 minutes*
Total Time *3 hours 30 minutes*
Yield *10 servings*

—

Ingredients

2 cups 00 flour
2 large eggs plus 6 egg yolks, beaten
1/4 cup extra-virgin olive oil, divided
Kosher salt, to taste
1 pound rigatoni pasta, cooked al dente according to package instructions
2 cups marinara sauce, plus more to serve
12 hard-boiled eggs, sliced in half lengthwise
12 meatballs, fully cooked
1 pound low moisture mozzarella, cut into 1/2-inch rounds
1/2 pound aged provolone, grated
1 pound Genoa salami, sliced into rounds

Preheat oven to 375°F.

In the bowl of a stand mixer fitted with a dough hook, add the flour, eggs, 2 tablespoons olive oil and salt to taste. Mix on low speed until a dough begins to form. Increase speed to medium-high and knead for 5 minutes or until smooth. Wrap in plastic wrap and leave out to rest for 30 minutes.

Brush the interior of a Dutch oven with the remaining 2 tablespoons olive oil. Unwrap dough and dust with flour. On a well-floured work surface, roll out dough into one large disc, about ⅛-inch thick. Roll dough around the rolling pin and unroll into the Dutch oven, carefully pressing down to the bottom, making sure to have about 6 inches or more hanging outside the vessel on all sides.

Start filling the timpano with a layer of cooked pasta tossed in a small amount of sauce. Begin forming layers using half of each of the fillings: eggs, then meatballs, cheeses, and salami. Repeat, starting with the pasta every time, until the Timpano is filled to the brim. Finish with a final layer of provolone. Carefully fold the excess dough up from the sides to cover the top and press down to seal shut.

Cover the Dutch oven and bake for 1½ hours. For a crispier crust, bake uncovered. Let the Timpano rest in the pot for one hour, then place a large cutting board over top and invert. Cut into slices, like you would a cake. Serve with a spoonful of marinara sauce.

Slow Cooker Beef Ragu Pappardelle

Active Time *30 minutes*
Total Time *6 hours 30 minutes*
Yield *6 servings*

—

Ingredients

2 1/2 pounds beef chuck, cut into 4 large chunks
Kosher salt and freshly ground black pepper
2 tablespoons olive oil
1 yellow onion, diced
1 medium carrot, peeled and diced
1 stalk celery, diced
5 cloves garlic, minced
2 teaspoons fresh thyme, roughly chopped
1 bay leaf
3 tablespoons tomato paste
1 cup dry red wine
1 (28-ounce) can whole plum tomatoes, crushed by hand
16 ounces pappardelle, cooked al dente according to package instructions
Chopped parsley, to serve
Shaved Parmesan cheese, to serve

Turn slow cooker on high heat to warm.

Season beef on all sides with salt and pepper. In a large heavy-bottomed skillet over medium-high heat, add olive oil. Once the oil is hot, add the beef and brown on all sides for about 6 to 7 minutes. Remove to slow cooker.

Add onion, carrots, celery, garlic, thyme and bay leaf to the skillet, and stir until onions are translucent and vegetables are soft and fragrant, about 5 minutes. Season with salt and pepper and stir in tomato paste. Stir in red wine to deglaze the pan and stir up any browned bits on the bottom. Cook until wine is reduced, the pan is almost dry, and no longer has the sharp smell of alcohol. Stir in the tomatoes and let come to a light simmer.

Pour the tomato mixture over the beef in the slow cooker. Cover with a lid, and cook on low for 6 hours. Shred the beef in the slow cooker with 2 forks and mix all together to combine.

Toss pasta with about 2 cups of sauce. Serve pasta in bowls with more ragu spooned over the top, sprinkled with parsley and shaved Parmesan.

Bread

Bread is the best accessory to any meal, and nothing beats
the simple, but grand, pleasure of breaking bread — whether
you're with friends, family or flying solo! Try a sweet recipe
for a comforting breakfast or afternoon snack, and bake any
of these savory recipes for a feast with friends.

Cinnamon Twist Bread

Active Time *30 minutes*
Total Time *2 hours*
Yield *about 10 servings*

—

Ingredients

FOR THE DOUGH:

3 tablespoons unsalted butter
1 1/4 cups whole milk
1 tablespoon active dried yeast
4 cups all-purpose flour
1/3 cup granulated sugar
1 teaspoon salt
2 large eggs

FOR THE FILLING:

1/2 cup unsalted butter, softened
1 cup light brown sugar
2 tablespoons cinnamon

FOR THE ICING:

2 tablespoons unsalted butter, softened
1 cup powdered sugar
2 tablespoons milk
1 teaspoon vanilla extract

MAKE THE DOUGH:
In a small saucepan over medium heat, add the butter and milk and stir until the butter is melted and the mixture is warm to the touch. Do not boil.

Remove from heat and set aside to cool for a few minutes until the mixture is lukewarm. Next, add the yeast, and stir to dissolve.

In the bowl of a stand mixer fitted with the dough hook attachment, combine the flour, sugar and salt. With the mixer running, slowly pour in the milk mixture, then add the eggs. Continue to mix for 5 to 7 minutes until the dough is smooth and elastic.

Place dough in a greased bowl and cover with plastic wrap. Leave to rise for 45 minutes or until doubled in size.

MAKE THE FILLING:
In a small bowl, stir together butter, sugar and cinnamon until well combined.

ASSEMBLE THE BREAD:
Once the dough has risen, preheat oven to 350°F and grease an 11-by-14-inch baking sheet with butter.

Roll out the dough into a large rectangle, roughly 12- by 14-inches. (Don't worry too much about exact measurements for this step.)

Spread the filling all over the rolled out dough, then fold a third of the dough into the center. Fold the remaining third, up and over the first third, like a letter, so you are left with a skinny rectangle in the middle of your work space. Rotate 90 degrees. Fold the bottom third of the rectangle up, then bring the top third down to cover it so you are finally left with a small square.

If the dough is getting warm at this point, place in the fridge to chill for 30 minutes.

Once the dough is ready to roll again, roll the square of dough out to a rectangle, 10- by 12-inches and about ¼-inch thick. (Don't worry if some of the filling is escaping at this point.)

With a knife or a pizza cutter, cut the dough into ¾-inch strips. Twist each strip a few times, then place onto the lined baking sheet so you have a sheet of twisted dough pieces lined up next to each other. Leave to rise for 20 minutes.

Place in the oven for 15 to 20 minutes, until the top is golden brown.

Allow the bread to cool on the baking sheet for 5 minutes, then invert onto a piece of plastic wrap with the top of the bread, as it was cooked, facing down. Starting from the short side, roll the bread up into a spiral. Wrap the bread in the plastic wrap, and allow to cool.

FROST THE BREAD:
In a medium bowl, whisk together butter, sugar, milk and vanilla. Generously frost the top of the cooled loaf. Cut into slices and serve.

Stuffed Fold Over Sandwiches

Active Time *30 minutes*
Total Time *2 hours 45 minutes*
Yield *12 sandwich breads*

—

Ingredients

FOR THE DOUGH:

1 tablespoon active dry yeast
1 1/2 cups water, room temperature
4 cups bread flour
4 tablespoons superfine sugar
3 tablespoons nonfat dry milk powder
1 tablespoon salt
1/2 teaspoon baking powder
1/2 teaspoon baking soda
1/3 cup vegetable shortening, room temperature
1/4 cup vegetable oil
1 large egg, beaten

FOR THE SANDWICHES:

12 slices mozzarella cheese
12 slices tomato
12 slices prosciutto, cut into 4 pieces
12 basil leaves
Olive oil, to taste
Large flake salt, to taste

MAKE THE DOUGH:

In the bowl of a stand mixer fitted with the dough hook attachment, combine yeast and water and allow yeast to bloom, approximately 5 minutes. Add flour, sugar, milk powder, salt, baking powder, baking soda and shortening. Mix on the lowest setting for 8 to 10 minutes until the dough comes together and forms a ball. Remove, place in a well-oiled bowl, and cover with a towel for up to 1 ½ hours or until the dough doubles in size.

Once risen, punch the dough down and turn out onto a floured work surface. Divide the dough into 12 balls and cover with plastic wrap. Allow to rest for 30 minutes.

Preheat oven to 350°F and line 2 baking sheets with parchment paper.

Uncover dough balls and roll into 12 4-inch discs. Brush a disc with vegetable oil and fold in half. Brush the half with vegetable oil and fold in half again, creating a triangle shape. Repeat with remaining balls, and place on the prepared baking sheets. Brush each triangle with egg wash, and bake for 15 to 20 minutes. Buns will be golden and spring back to the touch.

ASSEMBLE THE SANDWICHES:

Place a piece of cheese in one pocket of the bun, tomato and prosciutto in another and basil in the last. Drizzle with olive oil and sprinkle with salt. Repeat until all buns are stuffed.

Philly Cheesesteak Pastry Bombs

Active Time *60 minutes*
Total Time *2 hours 30 minutes*
Yield *4 rolls*

—

Ingredients

FOR THE DOUGH:

2 cups all-purpose flour
1 teaspoon sugar
1 teaspoon salt
1 teaspoon active dry yeast
2 tablespoons olive oil
1/2 cup milk, warmed
1/2 cup butter, melted
2 large eggs
2 tablespoons water

FOR THE FILLING:

2 tablespoons olive oil, divided
5 ounces sirloin steak, finely sliced
1 green pepper, diced
1 onion, diced
8 slices provolone cheese

MAKE THE DOUGH:

In a large bowl, add the flour, sugar, salt and yeast. Stir to mix, then slowly add in the oil and milk, stirring and mixing together. Knead to form a smooth dough, then cover and set aside to rest for 1 hour.

MAKE THE FILLING:

In a large frying pan over medium heat, heat 1 tablespoon of oil. Add the beef, and cook until browned all over. Remove from the heat and set aside in a bowl.

In the same frying pan, heat another tablespoon of oil, then add the onion and pepper. Cook for 5 minutes or until starting to soften. Tip into the bowl with the beef. Set aside to cool.

ASSEMBLE THE BUNS:

Preheat oven to 350°F. Line a baking sheet with parchment paper and grease with oil.

Uncover the dough, knead for 2 to 3 minutes then divide into 4 equal parts. Dust generously with flour, and roll out each piece into a very thin round circle. Stack them on top of each other as you go, and add a dusting of flour in between each circle of dough. Roll the stack out gently and slowly to make larger and thinner sheets.

One at a time, brush melted butter on the top surface of a round of dough, then flip over and add a quarter of the meat filling in the middle. Next, top with a quarter of the cheese. Close in the sides of the round sheet in your hand, gathering towards the center, and twist the bottom. Tuck the top half of the gathered dough down over the filled dough ball to create a pretty fan design. Repeat the same for remaining sheets.

Mix water and eggs together to create egg wash. Transfer the pies onto the baking pan, and brush with egg wash. Bake for 25 minutes, or until golden, then set aside to cool slightly. Buns are best served warm.

Savory Monkey Bread

Active Time *15 minutes*
Total Time *40 minutes*
Yield *about 10 servings*

—

Ingredients

6 tablespoons olive oil, plus more for garnish
1 red bell pepper, seeded and finely diced
Zest of 2 lemons
2 cloves garlic, minced
1/2 teaspoon paprika
1 1/2 cups Parmesan cheese, shredded and divided
3 tablespoons sesame seeds
1 tablespoon fresh oregano, minced, plus more for garnish
1 tablespoon fresh thyme, minced, plus more for garnish
1 tablespoon fresh marjoram, minced, plus more for garnish
1 1/2 tablespoons sumac
1 1/2 tablespoons ground cumin
1 1/2 tablespoons sesame seeds
1 teaspoon kosher salt
1 teaspoon pepper
2 (16-ounce) cans buttermilk biscuits
Sea salt, to garnish

Preheat oven to 375°F. Grease a Bundt pan with cooking spray.

Place olive oil in a small bowl. In a separate small bowl, mix red pepper, lemon zest, garlic and paprika. In another small bowl, place 1 cup of shredded cheese. In another small bowl place sesame seeds. In the final small bowl, mix together the oregano, thyme, marjoram, sumac, cumin, sesame seeds, salt and pepper.

Cut each round of biscuit dough in half and roll each half into a ball. Coat each ball with olive oil, then roll each ball in one topping, choosing cheese, sesame seeds, red pepper mix, or za'atar, and working in order so you fill the pan with alternating flavors throughout the loaf. Halfway through filling the pan, top the loaf with the remaining ½ cup of cheese. Continue until all dough balls are in the pan.

Bake for 25 to 30 minutes, or until loaf is golden brown. Let cool 5 minutes then turn out onto a plate and drizzle with olive oil, sea salt and fresh herbs. Serve alongside olive oil for dipping.

Pepperoni Meatball Bread Knots

Active Time *45 minutes*
Total Time *1 hour 5 minutes*
Yield *4 bread knots*

Ingredients

FOR THE GARLIC OIL:

1/4 cup extra-virgin olive oil
2 cloves garlic, minced

FOR THE MEATBALLS:

6 ounces pepperoni sausage
6 ounces (85/15) ground beef
1 large egg
1/4 cup Italian breadcrumbs
3 tablespoons chopped fresh basil
1/2 teaspoon red pepper flakes
1/2 teaspoon ground fennel
1/2 teaspoon dried Italian herbs
1/4 cup extra-virgin olive oil

FOR THE BREAD KNOTS:

3 tablespoons all-purpose flour
1 pound store-bought pizza dough, room temperature
1 cup shredded 4-cheese blend (Parmesan, Asiago, fontina and provolone)
1/2 cup tomato sauce, plus more to serve
Parmesan cheese, shredded
Flake salt

Place oven rack in the middle and preheat oven to 450°F. Put a large cast-iron skillet into the oven to preheat.

MAKE THE GARLIC OIL:
In a small bowl, add olive oil and garlic. Stir to combine and set aside to infuse.

MAKE THE MEATBALLS:
In the bowl of a food processor, add the pepperoni. Process until the pepperoni is finely ground. Remove into a large mixing bowl. Add the ground beef, egg, breadcrumbs, basil, red pepper flakes, fennel and Italian herbs. Using a fork, mash together the meatball mixture to evenly combine. Form the mixture into 4 even-sized meatballs.

In a medium nonstick skillet over medium-high heat, add the olive oil. Gently place the meatballs in the pan and cook for 3 to 4 minutes per side to sear (not fully cook). Remove the meatballs from the pan onto a plate to cool.

ASSEMBLE THE BREAD KNOTS:
Lightly dust a clean, flat work surface with flour. Roll the pizza dough out into a 12-inch circle and then cut into quarters. Put ¼ cup of shredded cheese in the middle of each piece of dough. Top with a meatball, 2 tablespoons tomato sauce and sprinkle with Parmesan. Enclose the meatball with the dough, gathering it at the top like a top knot. Tie the knot with butcher's twine. Using a pastry brush, coat the exterior of the knot with the infused garlic oil. Season with flake salt. Set aside on the floured surface and quickly assemble the remaining 3 knots in a similar fashion.

Carefully remove the heated cast-iron pan from the oven. Place the meatball knots onto the hot pan and return to the oven to bake for 15 to 20 minutes, until browned and the dough is fully cooked. Remove from the oven and allow to cool slightly. Serve with tomato sauce and Parmesan cheese.

Cream Cheese-Stuffed Pumpkin Rolls

Active Time *45 minutes*
Total Time *2 hours 15 minutes*
Yield *16 rolls*

—

Ingredients

1 (.25-ounce) envelope active dry yeast
1/2 cup whole milk, scalded and
allowed to cool to 110 degrees
1 teaspoon granulated sugar
1/3 cup brown sugar
4 tablespoons butter, softened
1 1/2 teaspoons kosher salt
2 teaspoons pumpkin pie spice
2 large eggs
1 cup pumpkin puree
4 cups all-purpose flour
8 ounces cream cheese, cut into 16
1/2-ounce blocks, chilled
20 pecan halves, sliced vertically into
thirds
1/3 cup butter, melted

In a small bowl, stir together yeast, milk and sugar. Allow the yeast to bloom for about 10 minutes until frothy.

In the bowl of a stand mixer fitted with the paddle attachment, add yeast mixture, brown sugar, butter, salt, spices, eggs, pumpkin puree and flour. Mix until well combined. Switch to the dough hook and knead dough for about 8 to 10 minutes, until smooth and soft. Place the dough in a greased bowl, cover with a linen and allow to rise for about 1 hour, or until doubled in size.

Divide the dough into 16 pieces. Fill each dough ball with a cube of cream cheese, pinch dough together to cover, then roll into a ball. Take a long piece of string and find the halfway point. Place the halfway point on top of the ball and flip the whole thing over. Pull the two pieces of string together and cross them over to create a cross on the bottom of the ball. Flip over again and do the same thing until the ball is segmented into 8 equal pieces, creating a pumpkin shape, taking care not to pull too tight as the dough will grow as it proofs and bakes. Tie the string at the top to secure and cut off any excess. Cover the pumpkin-shaped dough balls loosely and set them aside to proof until the dough is puffy and has doubled in size, about 1 to 1 ½ hours.

30 minutes before dough is ready to bake, preheat oven to 350°F.

Bake for 20 to 25 minutes, until cooked through and golden brown. Remove from oven and brush with melted butter. Allow rolls to cool slightly, then remove the twine and top with a vertically placed slice of pecan, meant to resemble a stem. Serve warm.

Leopard Print Bread Loaf

Active Time *50 minutes*
Total Time *4 hours 30 minutes*
Yield *1 9-by-5-inch loaf*

—

Ingredients

FOR THE BREAD STARTER:

2 tablespoons plus 2 teaspoons bread flour
1/4 cup whole milk
1/4 cup water

FOR THE BREAD DOUGH:

2 1/2 cups bread flour
1/4 cup sugar
1 packet active dry yeast
1 teaspoon salt
1 large egg
1/2 cup whole milk, warmed
4 tablespoons unsalted butter, room temperature
1/3 cup cocoa powder
1 tablespoon milk plus 1 teaspoon milk, divided, plus more to glaze
1/3 cup dark cocoa powder
2 teaspoons espresso powder

MAKE THE STARTER:

In a small saucepan over low heat, whisk together flour, milk and water. Bring to a simmer, whisking continuously until mixture has thickened, about 6 to 8 minutes. Pour into a small heatproof bowl, cover with plastic wrap and set aside to cool slightly.

MAKE THE DOUGH:

In a large bowl, combine flour, sugar, yeast and salt; mix well. Add egg, warm milk and cooled starter mix. Knead the mixture until it comes together, and continue for another few minutes. Add butter and knead for another 10 to 15 minutes until the dough becomes uniformly smooth and springs back to the touch.

Divide the dough into two parts, one slightly larger than the other. Roll the larger portion into a smooth ball and place in a buttered bowl. Cover with plastic wrap.

Cut the remaining portion of dough into two pieces, one slightly larger than the other. Incorporate the cocoa powder and 1 tablespoon of milk into the larger piece, kneading until the dough becomes a uniform light brown color. Form the dough into a smooth ball, place into a buttered bowl, then cover with plastic wrap.

Incorporate the dark chocolate cocoa and espresso powders with the remaining teaspoon of milk into the remaining dough ball, kneading well until the dough becomes a uniform dark brown color. Form the dough into a smooth ball, place into a buttered bowl, then cover with plastic wrap. Allow all three doughs to rise until they have doubled in size, about 50 minutes.

FORM THE LOAF:
Butter a 9-by-5-inch loaf pan well.

Once doubled, remove each ball of dough from its bowl and, one at a time, punch them down. Portion each ball into seven equal parts, forming each into balls. Cover all of the dough with plastic wrap to keep it moist.

Take one of the light brown balls of dough and roll it out into a small rectangle about 8-inches long. Roll the long side of the rectangle up tightly to form a long log, taking care not to allow any air to become trapped inside. Next, take a dark brown dough ball and roll it into a rectangle the length of the light brown log. Wrap the dark brown rectangle around the light brown log to enclose; set aside. Finally, take an uncolored dough ball and roll into a rectangle about 9-inches long. Place the dark brown log inside of the rectangle, wrap with dough and stretch a bit if necessary to match the length of the pan. Place the log in the pan and continue with the remaining dough in the same fashion, forming logs of concentric pieces of dough. When all dough is formed and in the pan, cover the loaf pan in plastic wrap, set a sheet pan on top and set aside to rise for another 40 to 50 minutes. Halfway through the proof, preheat oven to 350°F.

When the dough has risen, remove the sheet pan and plastic wrap, brush the top of the loaf with milk and bake for 35 to 40 minutes. When loaf is done, remove from the oven and allow to cool in the pan for about 10 minutes, then turn out loaf and finish the cooling process on a wire rack for at least one hour before slicing and serving.

Desserts

Dessert is the one thing that truly separates a regular weeknight meal from one that deserves a celebration — not that you need a reason to enjoy dessert! There's plenty of debate surrounding the perfect treat — think indulgent tarts, fudgy cookies and pillowy soft-centered cakes. There's no doubt, however, as to the sheer joy they bring!

Pavlova with Raspberry Swirls

Active Time *30 minutes*
Total Time *3 hours*
Yield *8 servings*

—

Ingredients

FOR THE BERRY SAUCE:

6 ounces fresh raspberries
1 tablespoon superfine sugar

FOR THE MERINGUE:

6 large egg whites
1 cup superfine sugar
1/4 teaspoon vanilla extract
1 teaspoon cream of tartar

FOR THE PAVLOVA:

3/4 cup heavy cream
1 tablespoon superfine sugar
1/4 teaspoon vanilla extract
1 cup fresh raspberries
1 cup fresh strawberries
1 cup fresh blackberries

MAKE THE BERRY SAUCE:
In the bowl of a food processor, add raspberries and sugar. Process until smooth. Using a fine mesh sieve, strain into a bowl. Discard seeds and reserve berry puree.

MAKE THE MERINGUE:
Heat oven to 180°F. Line a sheet pan with parchment paper. With a pencil, trace a 9-inch circle using a plate as a guide. Flip parchment over.

In the bowl of a stand mixer fitted with the whisk attachment, add egg whites and beat until soft and foamy. With the mixer running, slowly add the sugar, a tablespoon at a time, until the mixture is thick and glossy with stiff peaks. Add the vanilla and mix until incorporated, then add the cream of tartar and mix until thick.

Spoon a layer of the meringue onto the parchment into the middle of the circle. Drizzle with some raspberry sauce and swirl it into the meringue with the aid of a toothpick. Pile another layer of meringue on top and form a slight dip in the center. Gently drizzle a few tablespoons of the raspberry puree around the top of the pavlova. Use the toothpick to create swirls, taking care not to overwork or the meringue will deflate.

Bake for 1 ½ hours. Turn off oven and keep the door closed. Cool for 1 hour. It should be crisp on the outside yet still soft on the inside. Cool completely before removing.

ASSEMBLE THE PAVLOVA:
In a chilled medium bowl, whip the cream with a hand mixer until thick, then add the sugar and vanilla. Beat until soft peaks form.

Spoon the whipped cream onto the top of the pavlova, filling the indentation, drizzle with remaining berry sauce and top with fresh berries.

Smoothie Cakes

—
Active Time   *15 minutes*
Total Time   *3 hours*
Yield   *1 6- or 7-inch tart*

Ingredients

FOR THE CAKE BASE:

1/2 cup walnuts
1/2 cup unsweetened, shredded coconut
6 Medjool dates, pitted
1 tablespoon coconut oil
Pinch of sea salt

FOR THE SMOOTHIE FILLING:

2 cups diced mango
1/2 cup chopped pineapple
1/2 cup coconut butter
2 tablespoons coconut oil
2 tablespoons maple syrup
2 teaspoons ground turmeric
1 tablespoon lemon zest
1 tablespoon lemon juice

FOR THE TOPPING:

Frozen mango shapes, to serve
Edible marigold and nasturtium flowers, to serve

Mango Pineapple

MAKE THE BASE:
In the bowl of a food processor, add walnuts and process until coarsely ground. Add coconut, dates, oil and salt and pulse until the mixture comes together. Press into the bottom of a 6- or 7-inch springform pan, and set aside in the refrigerator.

MAKE THE FILLING:
In a blender, add the mango, pineapple, coconut butter, coconut oil, maple syrup, turmeric, lemon zest and juice. Blend into a smooth puree. Pour mixture over the crust and freeze until set, about 2 ½ hours. Decorate with frozen mango cut outs and flowers.

Ingredients

FOR THE CAKE BASE:
1/2 cup walnuts
1/2 cup unsweetened, shredded coconut
6 Medjool dates, pitted
1 tablespoon coconut oil
Pinch of sea salt

FOR THE SMOOTHIE FILLING:
2 cups sliced banana
1/2 avocado, pitted
1/2 cup chopped pineapple
1 cup baby spinach
1/2 cup coconut butter
2 tablespoons coconut oil
2 tablespoons maple syrup
1 teaspoon spirulina powder
1 tablespoon lemon zest
1 tablespoon lemon juice

FOR THE DECORATION TOPPING:
Shredded coconut, to serve
Mint leaves, to serve

Banana Avocado

MAKE THE BASE:
In the bowl of a food processor, add walnuts and process until coarsely ground. Add coconut, dates, oil and salt and pulse until the mixture comes together. Press into the bottom of a 6- or 7-inch springform pan, and set aside in the refrigerator.

MAKE THE FILLING:
In a blender, add the banana, avocado, pineapple, spinach, coconut butter, coconut oil, maple syrup, spirulina, lemon zest and juice. Blend into a smooth puree. Pour mixture over the crust and freeze until set, about 2 ½ hours. Decorate with shredded coconut and mint leaves.

Rhubarb Flower Tarts

Active Time *30 minutes*
Total Time *1 hour 20 minutes*
Yield *12 tarts*

—

Ingredients

FOR THE RHUBARB:

6 to 8 stalks fresh rhubarb
3 tablespoons sugar
Juice of 4 blood oranges
1 vanilla bean, split in half lengthwise

FOR THE TARTS:

1 1/2 cups white chocolate, melted
12 (3-inch) mini tart shells
2 cups lemon curd
Mint leaves, to garnish (optional)

ROAST THE RHUBARB:
Preheat oven to 400°F.

Using a vegetable peeler, shave rhubarb lengthwise into 3-inch long strips.

Place the shaved rhubarb into a medium baking dish and sprinkle with sugar. Pour in the juice and add the vanilla bean. Roast for 18 to 20 minutes. The rhubarb should be just soft. Allow the rhubarb to cool completely.

ASSEMBLE THE TARTS:
Fill each tart shell with a tablespoon of white chocolate. Form the rhubarb petals by taking a slice of rhubarb and bending it into a petal shape. Press it into the white chocolate and repeat 5 additional times per tart. Once set into the chocolate, pipe the lemon curd into the rhubarb petals. Place mint leaves, if desired, like leaves on the tarts. Serve immediately.

Banoffee Pie

Active Time *40 minutes*
Total Time *1 hour 50 minutes*
Yield *1 9-inch pie*

—

Ingredients

FOR THE CRUST:

2 cups graham cracker crumbs
6 tablespoons butter, melted

FOR THE FILLING:

3/4 cup butter
1/2 cup dark brown sugar
3 cups sweetened condensed milk
3 large bananas
2 cups heavy cream, chilled
1 tablespoon light brown sugar
1/2 cup caramel sauce
1/2 cup chocolate sauce

MAKE THE CRUST:
Preheat oven to 325°F.

In a medium bowl, mix together graham cracker crumbs and melted butter until moistened and mixed through. Press mixture into the bottom and sides of a 9-inch deep-dish pie tin. Bake for 10 minutes until golden brown and fragrant. Let cool.

MAKE THE FILLING:
In a large nonstick skillet, melt the butter and sugar, stirring constantly. Add the sweetened condensed milk and cook, stirring well, until the mixture has turned a caramel color and comes to a boil. Allow the mixture to boil for at least one full minute before taking it off the heat. Let cool slightly, then pour the toffee into the crust and chill for at least one hour, or until ready to serve.

When ready to serve, slice bananas into ¼-inch rounds, and cover the top of the toffee surface.

In a large chilled bowl, use a hand mixer or whisk to whip together the cream and brown sugar until stiff peaks form. Spread whipped cream all over the surface of the pie. Drizzle with caramel and chocolate sauce. Using a knife, ripple the sauces through the whipped cream.

Cut and serve slightly chilled.

Hummingbird Cake

Active Time *1 hour*
Total Time *4 hours*
Yield *1 9-inch cake*

—

Ingredients

FOR THE CAKE:

1 large pineapple, peeled
1 cup vegetable oil
1 cup sugar
3 large eggs
1 tablespoon vanilla extract
3 cups all-purpose flour
1 teaspoon baking soda
1 teaspoon salt
1 teaspoon cinnamon
2 cups mashed bananas, from about 4 ripe bananas
1 cup unsweetened shredded coconut
3 cups walnuts, toasted and chopped, divided

FOR THE FROSTING:

3 cups cream cheese, room temperature
1 cup butter, room temperature
1 cup powdered sugar
1 tablespoon lemon juice
2 teaspoons vanilla extract

MAKE THE PINEAPPLE FLOWERS:
Preheat oven to 200°F and spray the back of a muffin tin with cooking spray.

Cut the pineapple in half crosswise and reserve half for the cake. Remove the eyes from the remaining half with a melon baller and then cut into extremely thin rounds, about 8 to 10 slices. Place pineapple slices on the back of the prepared muffin tin cups and bake for 45 to 50 minutes until the tops appear to be dried out. Remove tin from oven and flip slices into the muffin cups. Bake for another 20 minutes. Allow to cool completely inside of the muffin cups.

BAKE THE CAKE:
Turn oven temperature up to 350°F. Grease 3 9-inch cake pans with cooking spray and line with parchment paper.

Chop remaining pineapple into ¼-inch pieces, removing the core.

In a large bowl, beat oil and sugar until thickened, about 2 minutes. Add eggs, one at a time, then add vanilla. Stir in flour, baking soda, salt and cinnamon, mixing until combined. Gently fold in chopped pineapple, bananas, coconut and one cup of the walnuts. Pour into prepared pans and bake for 35 to 40 minutes, or until a toothpick inserted into the center of the cakes comes out clean. Allow to cool.

MAKE THE FROSTING:
In a large bowl, beat cream cheese until light and fluffy. Add butter and mix until thoroughly combined. Stir in powdered sugar until smooth. Add lemon juice and vanilla.

ASSEMBLE THE CAKE:
Start by placing one cake layer on a cake stand and top with ½ cup frosting. Spread to form an even layer and top with another cake. Repeat until all cakes are used. Cover cake with half of the remaining frosting and place in the fridge for 20 minutes to form a crumb coat. Retrieve from the fridge and cover the top and sides of the cake with the last of the frosting. Around the sides of the cake, decorate with the remaining two cups walnuts. Place pineapple flowers around the top edge and serve.

Oreo Churros

Active Time *35 minutes*
Total Time *1 hour*
Yield *about 6 churro sandwiches*

—

Ingredients

FOR THE CHURROS:

10 chocolate-crème sandwich cookies, like Oreos
1 cup all-purpose flour
1/4 cup extra dark cocoa powder
1 teaspoon salt
1 cup water
1/2 cup unsalted butter
2 large eggs
1/2 cup sugar

FOR THE CREME FILLING:

1/2 cup unsalted butter, softened
1/2 cup vegetable shortening
1 teaspoon vanilla extract
3 cups powdered sugar, sifted

MAKE THE CHURROS:

Preheat oven to 425°F and line 2 baking sheets with parchment paper.

Separate sandwich cookie fillings from the cookies and place into 2 separate bowls. In the bowl of a food processor, grind cookies until the texture resembles sand. Reserve the crème for the filling.

In a small bowl, sift together flour, cocoa, salt and cookie crumbs.

In a small saucepan over medium heat, combine water and butter. Bring to a simmer until butter is melted. Turn off heat and add flour mixture, mixing until combined. Stir in eggs. Transfer to a pastry bag fitted with a ½-inch star tip.

Pipe the dough into 2 ½-inch circles on the prepared baking sheets, starting at the center of the circle and working outward in a spiral pattern. You should get about 12 circles. Bake for 20 to 25 minutes until slightly crispy. Once slightly cooled, toss churros in sugar; set aside.

MAKE THE FILLING:

In the bowl of a stand mixer fitted with the paddle attachment, cream butter, shortening and vanilla on high speed until light and fluffy. Gradually add powdered sugar on low speed, then add in the crème filling from the cookies. Transfer to a pastry bag fitted with a round tip.

ASSEMBLE THE CHURROS:

Turn half of the churro cookies over, and pipe a layer of filling onto them. Top with the other half of the churro cookies.

Baklava Tartlets

Active Time *35 minutes*
Total Time *5 hours 10 minutes*
Yield *12 tarts*

—

Ingredients

FOR THE BAKLAVA TARTS:

1/2 cup pistachios, plus more to garnish
1 1/2 cups walnuts
1/2 cup almonds
1/3 cup sugar
1 teaspoon cinnamon
1 pound phyllo dough, thawed
3/4 cup melted butter

FOR THE SYRUP:

3/4 cup water
3/4 cup sugar
3/4 cup honey
1 tablespoon lemon zest
2 tablespoons lemon juice
1 1/2 teaspoons orange blossom water

MAKE THE TARTS:
Preheat oven to 350°F.

In the bowl of a food processor, add the pistachios, walnuts, almonds, sugar and cinnamon and pulse until finely chopped and uniform in size.

Cut out 24 4 ½-inch squares and, using a round cutter, 72 3-inch rounds of phyllo, taking care to keep the dough covered with a damp paper towel so as not to dry out. Brush the phyllo squares with melted butter and place 2 squares into each muffin tin. Fill each with a spoonful of the nut mixture and a round or two of phyllo; brush with butter. Repeat until tins are completely full, brushing each round of phyllo as you go. Bake for 30 to 35 minutes, or until golden brown.

MAKE THE SYRUP:
While the baklava bakes, in a small saucepan, combine water, sugar, honey, lemon zest, lemon juice and orange blossom water. Bring to a boil and allow to reduce for about 10 minutes. Let cool, then spoon over the baklava tarts, hot out of the oven.

Leave to set at room temperature for about 4 hours. Garnish with crushed pistachios before serving.

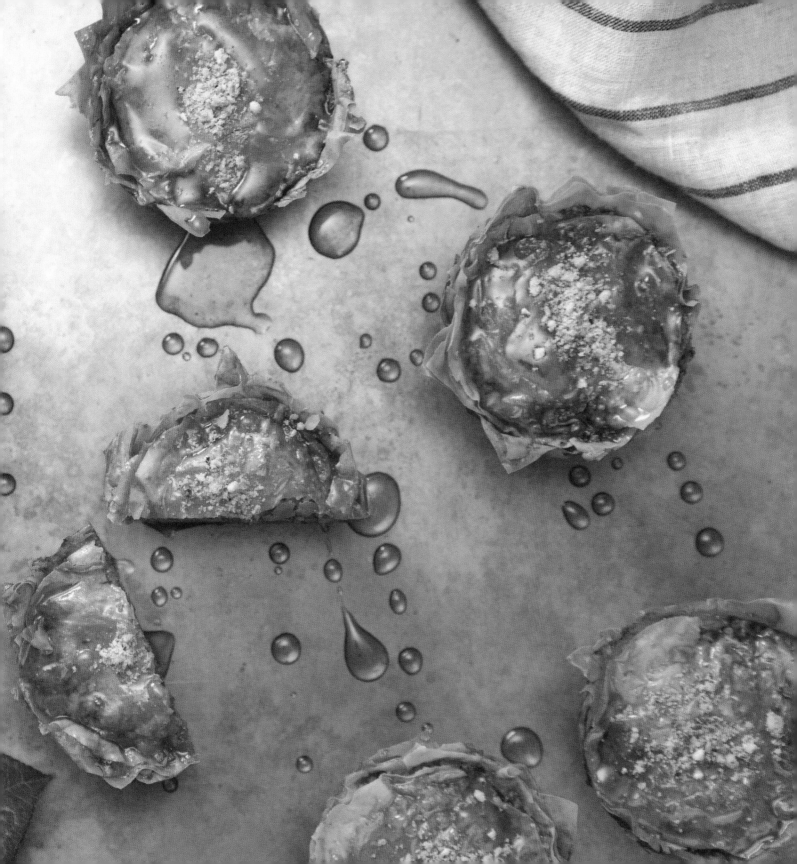

Peach Cookies

Active Time *40 minutes*
Total Time *2 hours 15 minutes*
Yield *24 cookies*

—

Ingredients

FOR THE PASTRY CREAM:

1 3/4 cups whole milk
Rind of one lemon, cut in strips
4 large egg yolks
3/4 cup sugar
1/4 cup all-purpose flour
1 teaspoon Luxardo liqueur

FOR THE COOKIES:

4 cups all-purpose flour
1 tablespoon baking powder
3 large eggs
1 3/4 cup sugar, divided
2 tablespoons peach schnapps
3/4 cup whole milk
1 stick unsalted butter, melted
Food coloring, yellow and peach colored
1 1/2 cups Luxardo liqueur
Mint leaves

MAKE THE PASTRY CREAM:

In a small saucepan over low heat, add milk and lemon rind. Warm until the milk is infused with lemon flavor, about 10 minutes, then remove rind.

In a large bowl, whisk together the egg yolks and sugar, then whisk in the flour. Slowly incorporate the warm milk, then pour mixture back into the saucepan and cook over low heat, stirring constantly, until mixture is bubbling and thick. Remove from heat and whisk in liqueur.

Pour into a heatproof bowl, cover with a layer of plastic wrap touching the surface to keep a skin from forming, and refrigerate until chilled.

BAKE THE COOKIES:

Preheat oven to 350°F and line a baking sheet with parchment paper.

In a medium bowl, sift together flour and baking powder.

In a large bowl, whisk together eggs and ¾ cup sugar until combined, then add peach schnapps, milk and butter. Whisk until incorporated, then carefully mix in the flour and baking powder mixture. The dough will be thick. Mix with a fork until the dough is smooth, then let rest for 10 minutes. Form into smooth balls about 1 tablespoon in size and place on the prepared baking sheet.

Bake for about 15 minutes until just golden. Let cool slightly, then while still warm use a paring knife to cut a teaspoon-sized indentation into the flat side of each cookie. Set aside to cool completely.

ASSEMBLE THE COOKIES:

Sort cooled cookies into halves that match one another, then fill each flat side with pastry cream. Sandwich the two sides together. Run a finger along the seam of the peach to seal the two cookies together. Place aside to set.

Place remaining 1 cup sugar in a small bowl. Fill two small bowls with ¾ cup of Luxardo each. Add yellow food coloring to one and peach food coloring to the other, then mix well.

Dip one side of a sandwiched cookie in the yellow-tinted liqueur, then dip the rest of the cookie in the peach-tinted liqueur. Roll the dipped cookie in the sugar bowl, coating all sides. Refrigerate until ready to serve. The cookies will taste even better in a few hours, after the liqueur flavor infuses. Before serving, insert a mint leaf into the center of the cookies to resemble a peach leaf.

Chocolate Caramel Crepe Cake

Active Time *1 hour 30 minutes*
Total Time *2 hours 30 minutes*
Yield *1 9-inch cake*

—

Ingredients

FOR THE CHOCOLATE CAKE:

2 1/4 cups all-purpose flour
1 1/2 cups sugar
1/2 cup cocoa powder
1 1/2 teaspoons baking soda
3/4 teaspoon salt
1 1/2 cups water
3/4 cup canola oil
2 teaspoons vanilla extract

FOR THE CHOCOLATE FROSTING:

1 1/2 cups butter, softened
5 cups powdered sugar, sifted
1 cup cocoa powder, sifted
1/2 cup milk
2 teaspoons vanilla extract

FOR THE CREPES:

5 cups all-purpose flour
10 large eggs
2 1/2 cups milk
2 1/2 cups water
1/2 cup unsalted butter, melted

FOR THE CARAMEL SAUCE:

2 cups sugar
1/2 cup water
1 cup heavy cream, warmed
4 tablespoons butter

MAKE THE CHOCOLATE CAKE:
Preheat oven to 350°F and grease 3 9-inch round cake pans.

In a medium bowl, whisk together the flour, sugar, cocoa powder, baking powder and salt.

In a separate bowl, whisk together the water, oil and vanilla. Slowly add the wet ingredients into the dry ingredients, whisking all the while. Take care not to over mix.

Divide the batter evenly between the prepared pans. Bake for about 25 minutes, or until a toothpick inserted into the center comes out clean. Allow to cool completely, then level off the tops to create a flat surface.

MAKE THE CHOCOLATE FROSTING:
In the bowl of a stand mixer fitted with the paddle attachment, beat butter on high for about 3 minutes, or until it has turned pale in color and is light and fluffy. Add half of the powdered sugar and cocoa powder and mix until incorporated. Add the remaining sugar and cocoa powder and beat on high. Add the milk and vanilla extract. Mix until well combined, then set aside.

MAKE THE CREPES:
Whisk the flour and eggs in a mixing bowl until well incorporated. Mix in the the milk and water. Add the butter and beat until the mixture is completely smooth.

Heat a lightly oiled 9-inch crepe pan over medium heat. Pour in approximately 3 tablespoons of batter, just enough to line the bottom. Let cook for approximately 2 minutes, flip and cook the other side for 2 minutes. Transfer finished crepe to a large plate. Repeat until batter is gone and about 30 crepes have been made.

MAKE THE CARAMEL SAUCE:
In a medium saucepan over medium-high heat, combine the sugar with the water and stir to combine. Cook, without stirring, until the sugar has turned a deep amber hue, approximately 10 to 12 minutes.

Carefully add the heated cream, whisking quickly to combine. Simmer for 2 minutes and take off the heat. Whisk in butter and allow to cool to room temperature.

ASSEMBLE THE CAKE:
Place a layer of cake on a cake stand and coat the top with a thin layer of caramel sauce. Place a crepe on top, coating with a thin layer of sauce. Repeat this step 15 times, and carefully trim any crepe edges that stick out past the circumference of the cake. Repeat this process with another cake layer on another cake stand. Once both cakes have been layered with 15 crepes, stack one on top of the other, and top the stack with the remaining cake layer.

Chill in fridge about 15 minutes so the caramel can solidify. Apply a thin crumb coat of frosting to the top and sides of cake, and chill an additional 15 minutes. Apply another coat of frosting to the cake and smooth out to get a clean appearance. Drizzle the remaining caramel on top and let drip down the sides.

Cookie Dough Ice Cream Cone Cakes

Active Time *45 minutes*
Total Time *1 hour 35 minutes*
Yield *12 cake cones*

—

Ingredients

FOR THE BATTER:

12 waffle ice cream cones
1 pint cookie dough ice cream, thawed at room temperature
1 1/2 cups self-rising flour

FOR THE CAKES:

1 pint cookie dough ice cream, frozen
1 pint edible cookie dough, chilled
4 cups vanilla buttercream
2 cups dark chocolate, melted
Mini cookies, to garnish
Whipped cream, to garnish

BAKE THE BATTER:

Preheat oven to 350°F and place the rack in the lower third of the oven. Line 12 cupcake tins with a large square sheet of tin foil. Place 1 cone in the center of each cupcake mold and form the foil around the cone so it stands upright and is secure and stable.

In a medium bowl, mix the thawed ice cream and flour until combined. Fill the ice cream cones with the batter, about two-thirds of the way up the cones. Bake for 15 to 18 minutes, or until a skewer inserted into the center of the cakes comes out clean. Allow to cool completely.

ASSEMBLE THE CAKES:

Scoop one small scoop of ice cream into a cooled cone. Top with one small scoop of cookie dough. Fill a piping bag with buttercream and pipe the top in an ice cream-swirl fashion, covering the ice cream and cookie dough. Place in the freezer for 15 minutes. Dip the top of the cone into the melted chocolate and top with mini cookies and whipped cream. Serve immediately or keep frozen.

Easy Fraisier Cake

Active Time *35 minutes*
Total Time *3 hours 30 minutes*
Yield *8 to 10 servings*

—

Ingredients

*1 box white cake mix, prepared
according to package instructions
2 pints strawberries, trimmed
4 (8-ounce) packages cream cheese,
softened
1 (14-ounce) can sweetened condensed
milk
1 teaspoon vanilla extract
1/4 cup lemon juice
1 1/2 cups whipped cream
Mint leaves, to garnish
Strawberry jam, to garnish*

Bake the cake mix batter in two 8-inch round pans. Allow to cool completely, then level off the tops of the cake.

Slice about 10 strawberries in half lengthwise and set aside.

Use an acetate strip to form a collar around an 8-inch cake board; tape it closed. Place a cake layer at the bottom of the acetate. Place the strawberries, cut-side facing outwards, around the edge of the acetate. The strawberry halves should be sitting snugly beside each other, so it looks like a crown around the edge of the cake.

In a large bowl, use a hand mixer to cream the cream cheese. Slowly add in condensed milk, vanilla and lemon juice. Pour over the cake and strawberries; smooth the top. Place the cake in the fridge and allow to set for 3 hours.

When ready to serve, fill a piping bag with whipped cream. Remove cake from fridge and peel acetate collar away from the edges. Pipe whipped cream dollops in concentric circles around the top of the cake, starting from the outer edge and working your way inwards. Top with thinly sliced strawberries and mint leaves. Serve immediately, with strawberry jam if desired.

NOTE: *This recipe uses only 1 of the 2 layers of cake. The additional layer can be wrapped in plastic wrap and frozen to wait for another use. Thaw before using.*

Black Sesame Zebra-Striped Cheesecake

Active Time *20 minutes*
Total Time *3 hours 40 minutes*
Yield *1 6-inch cake*

—

Ingredients

FOR THE CRUST:

5 chocolate-crème sandwich cookies, like Oreos
1/4 cup pecans
2 tablespoons butter, melted

FOR THE CHEESECAKE FILLING:

3 teaspoons powdered gelatin
2 tablespoons water
3 tablespoons black sesame paste
1 (8-ounce) package cream cheese
3/4 cup cream
1/2 cup plain yogurt
1/2 cup milk
4 tablespoons granulated sugar
1 tablespoon lemon juice
Whipped cream, to serve
Mint, to serve
Black sesame seeds, to serve

MAKE THE CRUST:
Line the bottom of a 6-inch springform pan with parchment paper.

Add cookies and pecans to a plastic zip top bag. Use a rolling pin to crush into small pieces. Transfer to a medium bowl and add melted butter. Combine until moistened and mixed through, then transfer to the prepared pan. Press down to form the crust. Refrigerate until set, about 20 minutes.

MAKE THE CHEESECAKE:
In a small microwave-safe bowl, sprinkle the gelatin over the water and let it bloom. Heat dissolved gelatin in the microwave at 500 watts for 30 seconds. Stir in sesame paste.

In a blender, add cream cheese, cream, yogurt, milk, sugar and lemon juice. Blend until smooth and well combined, then divide mixture between 2 bowls. Add sesame mixture to one of the bowls and whisk to combine until batter is gray in color.

Use an ice cream scoop to dollop scoopfuls of the batter in the center of the crust, alternating between white and gray until all the batter is used up. Refrigerate until set, about 3 hours.

To serve, garnish with whipped cream, mint and black sesame seeds.

Raspberry Lemonade Cookie Tarts

Active Time *1 hour*
Total Time *3 hours*
Yield *12 tarts*

—

Ingredients

FOR THE LEMONADE COOKIE DOUGH:

2 cups all-purpose flour
3/4 teaspoons baking powder
1/2 teaspoon kosher salt
1/2 cup plus 2 tablespoons butter, chilled and cubed
1 large egg
6 tablespoons sugar
2 tablespoons lemon zest

FOR THE RASPBERRY COOKIE DOUGH:

2 cups all-purpose flour
3/4 teaspoons baking powder
1/2 teaspoon kosher salt
3 tablespoons freeze-dried raspberry powder
1/2 cup plus 2 tablespoons butter, chilled and cubed
6 tablespoons sugar
1 large egg

FOR THE TARTS:

12 raspberry-filled thumbprint cookies
1/4 cup white chocolate, melted
1 cup lemon curd
1 pint fresh raspberries

MAKE THE LEMONADE COOKIES:
In the bowl of a food processor, add flour, baking powder and salt and pulse to combine. Add butter, egg, sugar and zest. Pulse until the mixture comes together. Turn out onto a surface, form the dough into a disk, wrap in plastic wrap and chill in fridge 20 minutes.

MAKE THE RASPBERRY COOKIE:
In the bowl of a food processor, add flour, baking powder, salt and freeze-dried raspberry powder and pulse to combine. Add the butter, sugar and egg and pulse until the dough comes together. Turn out onto a surface, form the dough into a disk, wrap in plastic wrap and chill in fridge 20 minutes.

Preheat oven to 375°F and grease a mini donut pan with cooking spray.

Remove the dough disks from the fridge, and form into small ¾-inch circle petals. Place the petals into the pan, alternating raspberry and lemon petals, and overlapping the edges. Gently press the dough into the pan and chill for 15 minutes.

Bake for 7 to 9 minutes. Allow to cool slightly, then remove from pan and cool completely.

ASSEMBLE THE COOKIE TARTS:
Dip the top of a raspberry thumbprint cookie into the melted white chocolate and place the flower cookie on top. Allow to set, then fill the center with about two tablespoons lemon curd, and top with a raspberry in the center. Repeat with all cookies. Serve immediately.

Triple-Decker Mississippi Mud Pie

Active Time *45 minutes*
Total Time *6 hours*
Yield *1 9-inch pie*

—

Ingredients

FOR THE CRUST:

*60 chocolate wafer cookies (from about 2
1/2 9-ounce packages)*
1/2 cup butter, melted
1 teaspoon salt

FOR THE CAKE:

1/4 cup coffee
1 cup dark brown sugar
*13 ounces dark chocolate (about 70%
cacao), chopped*
1 cup butter, cubed
5 large eggs, separated
1 teaspoon vanilla extract

FOR THE CHOCOLATE
PUDDING:

3/4 cup sugar
1/2 cup dark cocoa powder
1/4 cup cornstarch
1/2 teaspoon salt
4 large egg yolks
2 1/2 cups whole milk
3 tablespoons butter
*3 ounces dark chocolate (about 70%
cacao), chopped*
2 teaspoons vanilla extract

FOR THE PIE:

2 cups whipped cream
1 cup chocolate shavings

Preheat oven to 350°F. Line a 9-inch springform pan with parchment paper. Line the edges with aluminum foil, creating a taller cake pan, approximately 8 inches tall.

MAKE THE CRUST:
In the bowl of a food processor, pulse chocolate wafers until they resemble course sand. Add butter and salt and pulse to combine. Press into the bottom and nearly all the way up the sides of the prepared pan; set in the freezer for 15 minutes. Bake for 10 minutes, then allow to cool.

MAKE THE CAKE:
In a small saucepan over medium-low heat, combine coffee and brown sugar; stir together until melted.

In a medium bowl, combine chocolate and butter. Pour coffee mixture over chocolate and stir until melted and completely smooth. Add egg yolks and vanilla and allow to cool completely.

In another bowl, whisk egg whites until stiff. Working in batches, fold whites into the chocolate mixture. Pour into the tin over the crust and bake until cake is barely set, about 30 to 35 minutes. Remove from oven and allow cake to cool completely. Chill, covered, in fridge.

MAKE THE CHOCOLATE PUDDING:
In a medium saucepan, combine sugar, cocoa powder, cornstarch and salt. Add egg yolks and whisk until combined. Slowly add in whole milk and bring mixture to a boil, stirring constantly to prevent burning. Remove from heat and transfer to a large bowl. Stir in butter, dark chocolate and vanilla until smooth. Allow to cool and set, covered, in the fridge for up to 3 hours.

ASSEMBLE THE PIE:
When ready to serve, remove cake from fridge and top with chocolate pudding. Top with whipped cream and chocolate shavings. Serve immediately.

Beehive Honey Cheesecake

Active Time *30 minutes*
Total Time *3 hours*
Yield *1 9-inch cake*

—

Ingredients

FOR THE CRUST:

*48 chocolate wafer cookies (from 2
9-ounce packages), finely ground
Pinch of salt
1/2 cup butter, melted*

FOR THE CHEESECAKE:

*3 cups cream cheese, softened
2 tablespoons honey
1/4 cup sugar
3 large eggs
2 teaspoons vanilla extract
1 teaspoon lemon juice*

FOR THE HONEYCOMB LAYER:

3/4 cup melted caramel candy melts

FOR THE BEE DECORATIONS:

*1/2 cup yellow candy melts, melted
1/2 cup chocolate, melted
12 sliced almonds*

Preheat oven to 325°F and prepare a 9-inch springform pan with cooking spray.

MAKE THE CRUST:
In a large bowl, add chocolate cookies, melted butter and salt. Combine until moistened and mixed through. Press into the bottom of the pan and set in the fridge.

MAKE THE CHEESECAKE:
In a large bowl, beat cream cheese until fluffy. Add honey and sugar. Add in eggs, one at a time, until combined. Add vanilla and lemon juice, taking care not to overmix. Pour filling over crust; smooth top. Bake for 40 to 45 minutes until cheesecake is set. Remove from oven and let cool for 1 hour. Set in fridge, covered, for 4 hours or overnight until completely set.

MAKE THE HONEYCOMB LAYER:
Grease another 9-inch springform pan with cooking spray and line with parchment paper.

Pour melted candy melts into the base of the pan and, working quickly, top with a 12-by-12-inch piece of bubble wrap. Gently press bubble wrap into the chocolate and set aside until firm. Remove the sides of the springform pan and peel away the bubble wrap to reveal a disc molded to resemble honeycomb.

MAKE THE BEES:
Line a baking sheet with parchment paper.

Pour each of the melted chocolates into small pastry bags. Pipe about 6 1-inch ovals of candy melts onto the parchment paper. Pipe chocolate across the top to create the stripes of a bee. Place two dots at the top for eyes. Place two sliced almonds on either side to create the wings. Repeat until all the bees are made. Let harden.

ASSEMBLE THE CHEESECAKE:
Unmold set cheesecake from the pan and top with honeycomb layer. Arrange bees over top and serve.

Dulce de Leche Doughnuts

Active Time *30 minutes*
Total Time *2 hours*
Yield *about 13 doughnuts*

—

Ingredients

1 cup warm milk
2 teaspoons active dry yeast
1/4 cup sugar, divided
4 cups whole wheat flour
Pinch of salt
2 large eggs
1/4 cup butter, room temperature
1 teaspoon vanilla extract
1 cup powdered sugar
1 1/2 cups dulce de leche

In a small bowl, combine milk, yeast and a pinch of sugar.

In the bowl of a stand mixer fitted with the dough hook attachment, combine the flour, remaining sugar and a pinch of salt. Add the yeast mixture, eggs, butter and vanilla. Knead well for about 5 minutes until smooth and elastic.

Turn out dough onto a lightly floured surface, and roll out into a rectangle about ¼-inch thick. Using a 2-inch circular cutter, cut out circles of dough and place on a baking sheet. Sprinkle dough with flour, cover with a clean cloth and let rise in a warm location for 1 ½ hours.

Heat a few inches of oil in a large frying pan over medium heat until the oil comes to 365°F. Working in batches, as to not overcrowd the pan, fry the dough until golden on both sides, turning once. Remove from oil and drain on paper towels. Let oil come back up to 365°F between batches. Sprinkle with powdered sugar while still warm.

Using a paring knife, make a small cut in the side of each doughnut. Place dulce de leche in a piping bag and fill each doughnut. Dust again with powdered sugar, to serve.

Hot Chocolate Mousse Pie

Active Time *35 minutes*
Total Time *3 hours*
Yield *1 7- or 8-inch pie*

—

Ingredients

FOR THE CRUST:

2 cups finely ground chocolate cookie crumbs
7 tablespoons unsalted butter, melted

FOR THE HOT CHOCOLATE MOUSSE:

1 1/4 cups chopped dark chocolate (about 70% cacao)
Pinch sea salt
2 cups heavy cream, chilled, divided
2 tablespoons granulated sugar
2 (.73 ounce) packets hot chocolate mix

FOR THE MARSHMALLOW TOPPING:

2 cups granulated sugar, divided
1/2 teaspoon cream of tartar
1/2 cup water
4 large egg whites

MAKE THE CRUST:
Preheat oven to 350°F and line a 7- or 8-inch springform pan with parchment paper.

In a large bowl, combine cookie crumbs and butter until moistened and mixed through. Press the crust into bottom and three-quarters of the way up the sides of the pan. Bake for 10 minutes, then let cool.

MAKE THE HOT CHOCOLATE MOUSSE:
Combine chocolate and salt in a large bowl.

Heat ½ cup cream in a small saucepan over medium heat until boiling. Pour into the bowl of chocolate and let stand 5 minutes to melt chocolate before mixing to combine. Stir until glossy and smooth. Let cool slightly.

Meanwhile, in a large chilled bowl, add remaining 1 ½ cups cream. Using a hand or stand mixer, start on low speed, gradually bringing it up to high, and beat the cream until soft peaks have formed. Add sugar and beat just until stiff peaks form. Add in hot chocolate mix and beat to incorporate. Add the cooled melted chocolate mixture in 3 additions, gently folding to combine between each addition. Pour into crust, then chill, covered, in freezer for at least 2 hours to set.

MAKE THE MARSHMALLOW TOPPING:
About 20 minutes before serving, in a small saucepan over high heat, stir together 1 ½ cups sugar, cream of tartar and water. Bring to a boil, then turn heat to medium-low and let reduce slightly, without stirring, for 4 to 5 minutes.

Meanwhile, place egg whites in the bowl of a stand mixer fitted with the whisk attachment. Beat on medium-high until soft peaks form. Turn mixer to high and gradually add in remaining ½ cup sugar. Once combined, very carefully pour hot sugar syrup into egg whites. Beat for 5 to 10 minutes until the bowl of the mixer has cooled to the touch and the meringue is thick and glossy. Use immediately or the mixture will set.

ASSEMBLE THE PIE:
Remove pie from freezer and remove from springform pan. Spoon the marshmallow mixture on top of the pie. Use a kitchen torch to lightly toast the marshmallow topping to a golden hue before serving.

Peppermint Roll Cake Pops

Active Time *45 minutes*
Total Time *2 hours 30 minutes*
Yield *6 pops*

—

Ingredients

FOR THE CAKE:

1/2 cup cake flour
1/4 cup cocoa powder, sifted
1/4 teaspoon salt
1/2 cup sugar
3 large eggs
2 large egg yolks
4 tablespoons butter, melted and cooled
1 teaspoon vanilla extract
1 teaspoon peppermint schnapps

FOR THE ITALIAN MERINGUE BUTTERCREAM:

5 large egg whites
1 cup sugar
3 sticks butter, softened
1/4 teaspoon salt
1 teaspoon peppermint schnapps
2 to 3 drops red food coloring

FOR THE CAKE POPS:

6 cookie pop sticks
Dark chocolate, melted
1/2 cup crushed candy canes

BAKE THE CAKE:

Preheat oven to 450°F. Grease a 9-by-13-inch jelly roll pan and line with parchment paper.

In a medium bowl, sift together cake flour, cocoa powder and salt.

In a medium heatproof bowl, combine sugar, eggs and egg yolks. Place bowl over a hot water bath and cook, stirring constantly, until sugar has dissolved.

Transfer the mixture to the bowl of a stand mixer fitted with the whisk attachment and whisk well, until mixture is thick and light in color, about 6 minutes. Add in the flour mixture and gently fold to combine. Fold in butter, vanilla and peppermint schnapps.

Spread evenly in prepared pan. Bake for 6 minutes. Transfer to a cooling rack covered with a kitchen towel to cool completely.

MAKE THE BUTTERCREAM:

In a medium heatproof bowl, heat egg whites and sugar over a hot water bath, stirring until sugar is dissolved.

Transfer to the cleaned bowl of a stand mixer, fitted with the whisk attachment. Whisk for about 10 minutes, until lofty and pale in color. The meringue will hold stiff peaks when ready. Switch to the paddle attachment and slowly add in butter, a few tablespoons at a time, until all butter is incorporated. Beat in salt and peppermint schnapps.

Divide the frosting in half between two bowls and tint one half with red food coloring; transfer to separate piping bags. Pipe diagonal stripes over the top of the cake and roll it up into a log. Refrigerate for about an hour.

ASSEMBLE THE CAKE POPS:

Insert pop sticks into the cake, then slice between each to create 6 roll cake pops. Freeze each slice for about 30 minutes until firm. Dip the exterior edge of each cake in the chocolate and sprinkle with crushed candy canes. Allow to set before serving.

Lumberjack Cake

Active Time   *1 hour 30 minutes*
Total Time   *4 hours*
Yield   *1 7-inch cake*

—

Ingredients

FOR THE RED VELVET CAKE (DARK RED LAYER):

2 tablespoons cocoa powder
2 tablespoons red food coloring
2 1/2 cups all-purpose flour, sifted
1 teaspoon baking soda
1 teaspoon salt
1/2 cup butter, room temperature
1 1/2 cups sugar
2 large eggs
2 teaspoons vanilla extract
1 cup buttermilk
1 tablespoon vinegar

FOR THE VANILLA CAKE (RED LAYER):

2 1/2 cups all-purpose flour, sifted
1 1/2 teaspoons baking powder
1/2 teaspoon baking soda
1 teaspoon salt
3 large eggs
1 teaspoon vanilla extract
3/4 cup butter, room temperature
1 1/2 cups sugar
1 cup buttermilk
8 drops red food coloring

Preheat oven to 350°F. Spray 3 9-inch round cake pans with cooking spray and line with parchment paper.

MAKE THE RED VELVET CAKE:
In a small bowl, combine cocoa powder and red food coloring to form a paste.

In a small bowl, combine flour, baking soda and salt.

In the bowl of a stand mixer fitted with the paddle attachment, cream butter and sugar until light and fluffy. Add in eggs, one at a time. Add in vanilla and the cocoa mixture. Alternate between adding the flour mixture and the buttermilk, making sure to combine thoroughly after each addition, occasionally scraping down the sides of the bowl. Add vinegar and mix until batter is smooth. Pour batter into a prepared pan and bake for 25 to 30 minutes, or until a toothpick inserted into the center comes out clean. Set aside to cool.

MAKE THE VANILLA CAKE:
In a medium bowl, sift together the flour, baking powder, baking soda and salt.

In a small bowl, whisk together eggs and vanilla.

In the bowl of a stand mixer fitted with the paddle attachment, cream butter and sugar until light and fluffy. Add egg mixture. Alternate adding in the flour mixture and the buttermilk until completely combined. Stir in red food coloring to achieve a dark pink color. Pour batter into a prepared pan and bake for 25 to 30 minutes, or until a toothpick inserted into the center comes out clean. Set aside to cool.

MAKE THE CHOCOLATE CAKE:
In the bowl of a stand mixer fitted with the paddle attachment, combine the flour, sugar, baking powder, baking soda, salt and cocoa powder. Mix in the butter, eggs and vanilla. Fold in the sour cream. Pour batter into the remaining cake pan and bake for 25 to 30 minutes, or a until a toothpick inserted into the center comes out clean. Set aside to cool.

MAKE THE CHOCOLATE BARK:
Spread chocolate in a thin layer across a 18-by-13-inch piece of parchment paper. Lay another piece of parchment on top of the chocolate and smooth out. Roll the parchment paper lengthwise into a log and set in the fridge to harden.

FOR THE CHOCOLATE CAKE (DARK BROWN LAYER):

1 1/2 cups all-purpose flour, sifted
1 cup sugar
1 teaspoon baking powder
1/2 teaspoon baking soda
1 teaspoon salt
1/3 cup cocoa powder
3/4 cup butter, room temperature
2 large eggs
2 teaspoons vanilla extract
3/4 cup sour cream, room temperature

FOR THE CHOCOLATE BARK:

2 cups melted dark chocolate
2 tablespoons cocoa powder

FOR THE CREAM CHEESE FROSTING:

2 cups cream cheese, room temperature
1 cup butter, room temperature
1 cup powdered sugar, sifted
2 tablespoons vanilla extract
1 tablespoon lemon juice

FOR THE CHOCOLATE FROSTINGS:

3 1/3 cups powdered sugar
4 1/2 tablespoons cocoa powder
1/2 teaspoon sea salt
3 sticks unsalted butter, room temperature
4 ounces bittersweet chocolate, melted and cooled
2 ounces milk chocolate, melted and cooled
4 1/2 tablespoons buttermilk, divided

MAKE THE CREAM CHEESE FROSTING:
In a large bowl, cream together cream cheese and butter with an electric mixer until smooth. Mix in powdered sugar, lemon juice and vanilla until well-combined.

MAKE THE CHOCOLATE FROSTINGS:
Sift together the powdered sugar and cocoa powder into a large bowl. Add in salt and butter. Using an electric mixer, beat on high until fluffy.

Remove one third of the mixture to another bowl. Add bittersweet chocolate to the larger amount of frosting, mix on low speed until almost incorporated, then beat in 3 tablespoons buttermilk.

Add milk chocolate to the smaller amount of frosting, mix on low speed until almost incorporated, then beat in remaining 1 ½ tablespoons buttermilk.

ASSEMBLE THE CAKE:
When cakes are cool, level off the tops and divide each cake horizontally into two layers of even height. We will only be using 1 of the chocolate layers for this recipe. Using 5-inch and 2-inch round cutters, cut concentric circles out of the red velvet cake. Separate the pieces so you have a 7-inch ring, a 5-inch ring and a 2-inch circle. Repeat this process with the remaining red velvet layer, the vanilla cake layers and chocolate cake layer.

Assemble the first layer by placing the outside red velvet cake ring on a plate or cake stand. Insert the next chocolate cake ring and then the inner red velvet cake circle. Cover with a layer of dark chocolate frosting. Assemble the next layer by placing the outside vanilla cake ring on the cake. Insert the next red velvet cake ring and then the inner vanilla cake circle. Continue forming layers alternating the colors on the outside until the cake is 4 layers tall.

Cover the top of the cake with the cream cheese frosting and the sides with the milk chocolate frosting. With the milk chocolate frosting, pipe a swirl on top, starting from the center out to the edge, and blend in to resemble the rings of a tree.

Remove chocolate bark from the fridge, unroll, dust with cocoa powder and place around the edge of the cake to resemble bark.

Thank You...

A sincere and heartfelt thank you to everyone whose creativity and hard work made this publication possible - Paul Delmont, Robert Abilez, Emily Horng, Jaclyn Delory Wilson, Edward Coleman, Sarah Anne Bargatze, Sandra Tripicchio, Brianna Beaudry, Aidan Bradbury-Aranda, Robert Broadfoot, Anna Lee, Andrew Pollock, Gerardo Cagigal, Trinity Shi, Raquel Alessi, Megan Hubbell, Isla Murray, Rose Exall, Charlotte O'Connell, Skylar Thomson-Edberg, Dagne Aiken, David Boyle, Ellie Holland, Aaron Keeling, Aaron Trager, April Rankin, Fumie Kojima, Wakana Hosokawa, Saiko Suzuki, Midori Moniwa, Geraldine Martin-Coppola, Sam Booker, Gracelyn Park, Merce Muse, Nisha Sethi, Dantel Hood, Farooq Haider, Fernanda Picoloto, Eduardo Hardt, Alex Fouracre, Sean Jackson, Guillem Serrano, Diana Crisan and Emma Niles.

Beyond the people listed above, thanks are due to the teams who endlessly support them and enable the special moments that made this book possible.

A special thanks to all the Michaels. And thank you to all the other members of our Tastemade family, especially Larry, Joe, and Steven.

INDEX

BREAD

DESSERTS